Praise for
Escape the Lie

"Drawing from a wealth of ministry experience and stories that will move your heart, Walker Moore's *Escape the Lie* will give you practical tools for healthy family relationships. With the wit of a Will Rogers and insights of a C.S. Lewis, Walker brings a fresh perspective on the universal heart longing of man, one that needed to be written." —Brian Hobbs, Editor, the *Baptist Messenger*, a statewide newsjournal for Oklahoma

"Once again, as in *Rite of Passage Parenting*, God has given Walker tremendous insight into the Christian life. There is no greater accomplishment than to know and believe the love of God as our Father. And yet so many believers still struggle to receive His love. I will recommend this book to every person seeking to find an answer to the question 'Is there more to the Christian life?'"—Doug Bischoff, Ph.D., Next Generations minister, Houston's First Baptist Church

"Hearts are to be molded and shaped into something beautiful and open. Yet too often our hearts are shoved and shattered until we lock the pain deep inside. Walker is handing us a key to return to the heart that beats of beautiful again. With story and teaching, he leads us to Escape the Lie and walk in freedom. This is a journey of hope and healing that God longs to walk with us." —Gregg Matte, Senior Pastor, Houston's First Baptist Church and author of *I AM Changes Who i Am*

"Have you ever been tempted to perform on the outside and yet felt empty on the inside? Ever wondered whether people would still love you if they knew what was really in your heart? Ever gotten tired of trying to earn the attention and love of those you care about? My friend Walker Moore helps each of us to embrace the truth of God's unconditional, always-pursuing, thirst-quenching, perfect love that casts out all fear and allows us to escape the lies of our enemy and this world. This book helped me remember that my heart is now fully adopted by the perfect Father!"—Casey Cariker, Lead Pastor, Rejoice Church, Owasso, Oklahoma

"God used Walker Moore to change my life. His ministry has brought millions around the world to the true freedom that can only be found in our Heavenly Father. Walker's message is a GPS for the soul to help you navigate the awesome journey God has uniquely planned for you. Open this book, unfold the map of truth, escape the lie, and let the journey to freedom begin!"—Ryan Underwood, CEO & Chief Leadership Officer, TRI Leadership Resources

"In *Escape the Lie* Walker reminds us of how the devil is a liar. And he tries to pull us away from the love of our heavenly Father any way he can. That's why so many people end up buying into the lie of the Orphan Heart: *I don't have a Father who loves me. I'm not important. I don't matter.* If any of these describe you or someone you love, read this book. You'll gain some incredible insights into how to embrace the truth that will set you free. Take Walker's message to heart—so the Orphan Heart won't take you."—Bart Millard of MercyMe, Nashville, Tennessee

ESCAPE THE LIE

JOURNEY TO
FREEDOM
FROM THE
ORPHAN
HEART

WALKER MOORE
WITH MARTI PIEPER

randall house

Printed in the United States of America

ISBN 13: 9780892656851

Details in some anecdotes and stories have been changed to protect the identities of the persons involved.

Cover design by Mark Combs, www.DzinDNA.com

Published in association with Christopher Ferebee, Literary Agent, Corona, California.

"Give thanks to the God of heaven;
for His lovingkindness is everlasting."

Psalm 136:26

Escape the Lie:
Journey to Freedom from the Orphan Heart

Table of Contents

Acknowledgments

The message of escaping the Orphan Heart has come to me in bits and pieces. God has woven people in and out of my life to bring different aspects of truth that have shaped and molded it.

I would like to thank Kelly Nichols, who introduced to me the truth that we are the Father's favorite children. I would also like to thank Jack Frost, who touched Kelly's life and helped many others to understand the Orphan Heart. I am grateful for the life and ministry of Jeff Littleton, who brought me a piece of the truth on identity and left a lasting impact on my life.

I would like to thank Chris Robinette for championing the Orphan Heart message; Chris Ferebee for believing in my work; Mark Combs for translating my ideas into clear diagrams; Marti Pieper for her organizational skills; and the staff at Randall House, who made this message better. I am grateful to my wonderful staff at Awe Star Ministries (Cathy, Chad, Carol, Meridith, and Gerri) who picked up my work load and gave me the time I needed to meet deadlines. You are the best.

This message has also been honed by the many pastors, church members, and Awe Star missionaries who have given me the privilege of sharing it. God used your incredible response to its truths to move me to put them into print. You'll find many of your stories within these pages.

And of course, I thank my family: Cathy, Jeremiah, Erin, Caleb, Adrian, and Titus, who have not only survived my Orphan Heart but loved and supported me in spite of it. Every day, you give me a true picture of the Father's love.

. . . and Dad, I love you.

FOREWORD

I love finding out things I don't know about people. I've known my wife since we were in seventh grade, but I'm still finding out new things about her every day. Those surprises keep life fun and interesting.

You probably know a few things about me. I'm in a band called MercyMe, and we've been blessed with a few songs including "Word of God Speak" and "I Can Only Imagine."

What you may not know is that before there was MercyMe, there was the Awe Star Worship Band. Yours truly traveled with Walker Moore and Awe Star Ministries across the country and around the world. If you want to hear a good story, ask Walker about how I used his yellow rain slicker as a sled one afternoon in Switzerland.

But something else you may not know is that Walker Moore is an incredible Bible teacher. One of MercyMe's gold records hangs in its frame in Awe Star's office because of our love, respect, and admiration for both Walker and his lovely wife, Cathy.

Walker's *Escape the Lie* teaching is also new to me. But like the rest of his teaching, it makes sense out of things I've never understood. Walker reminds us of how the devil is a liar. And he tries to pull us away from the love of our heavenly Father any way he can. That's why so many people end up buying into the lie of the Orphan Heart: *I don't have a Father who loves me. I'm not important. I don't matter.*

Maybe you're someone who loves Jesus but, deep down inside, you know something is missing. Maybe you're someone who has trouble trusting God and other people. Or maybe you're someone with hurts from the past that have left you wounded, weary, and worried about the future.

If any of these describe you or someone you love, read this book. You'll gain some incredible insights into how to embrace the truth that will set you free and live the kind of abundant life Jesus promised.

Take Walker's message to heart—so the Orphan Heart won't take you.

Bart Millard
Nashville, TN

1—The Orphan Heart:
The biggest lie starts small.

"For me a father is nothing more than a character in a fairy tale. I know fathers are not like dragons in that fathers actually exist, but I don't remember feeling that a father existed for me. . . I don't say this out of self-pity, because in a way I don't miss having a father any more than I miss having a dragon. But in another way, I find myself wondering if I missed out on something important."—Donald Miller and John MacMurray, *To Own a Dragon: Reflections on Growing Up Without a Father*[1]

My Story

I loved my dad. Although he's been gone for several years now, I love him still.

For most of his life, Dad worked as a diesel mechanic. I noticed early on that there are two types. One is the "Tidy Tool" kind. His shop is immaculate, his tools neatly arranged, his workbench free of grease and clutter. The other is the type—well, like my dad. Grimy wrenches and parts of all shapes and sizes littered his workbench. A thick coating of oil-soaked sawdust covered the concrete floor.

One day when I was about nine years old, Dad's job took him out of town. I woke up that morning and told myself, "I want to do something special—really special—to please him." I decided to clean up the garage that doubled as his shop. I hurried out so I could take full advantage of his absence. I hoisted the tall can of gasoline and cautiously tipped it. An uneven stream poured into an old plastic pail.

I dipped the first tool. The transformation had begun.

Dip. Scrub. Rub. I repeated the process until each one of Dad's prized Crafts-man© tools shone as never before. Next, I tackled the bulky toolbox (also a Craftsman model). It didn't exactly sparkle after my attention, but at least it didn't grab onto any finger that touched it.

The workbench loomed. I took one of dad's scrapers (restored to its original stainless shine) and began to file away years of crud. Back and forth, back and forth. With each scrape I thought about my dad. I could almost see the smile creasing his leathery face. I could almost hear his voice praising "my son" and the "man's job" I had done that day.

Almost.

Bench cleaning accomplished, I tackled the floor. Scoop. Sweep. Scrape. My small muscles ached, but I pressed through the pain to finish my task. I don't know how many hours went by before I realized Dad would be home soon. I decided that even a grease-stained floor was a huge improvement. He couldn't help but be proud of his oldest boy.

Or could he?

Dad's battered blue pickup left clouds of dust as it made its way down our rural route and onto the long driveway. I stood waiting beside the workbench, my little chest puffed with pride.

The truck rolled to a stop. The door slammed. The big boots trudged across the driveway and up to the open door of the garage. He was home! I could almost hear the words I'd awaited all day.

Dad entered the garage and saw the workbench in its shining glory. He opened a drawer and took note of the sparkling tools inside. Next, he rubbed the sole of one boot back and forth as if to check for any grime left behind on the floor. Once again, I anticipated his delight.

Instead, he scowled. "It's about time you did something around here." Without another word, he turned and went into the house.

Another door slammed. My chest collapsed. The silent messages screamed their way into my heart.

Until the day Dad died, I never stopped trying to earn his love.

Slumped by my dad's sparkling workbench that day, I knew pain. I knew the words I'd longed to hear. I knew they hadn't come. But what I didn't know was that my dad's thoughtless response allowed a shadow to slip across my heart. This unnamed, unidentified *something* would dull my life and my perspective for years to come.

My wife saw the shadow. My sons did, too. And nearly everyone who knew me experienced its effects. It darkened every thought, every emotion, every relationship, and every one of my goals, but I never recognized its presence.

If I stood quietly, it crept out, so I unconsciously filled my life with noise and clutter. I feared silence because it gave the shadow an opportunity to reappear and whisper its words of hatred and deception. *You're no good. What made you think you could do that anyway? You always were the slow one!* And of course, *It's about* time *you did something around here.*

Do you have a similar story, a story of a painful relationship or experience that cast its shadow across your life? Maybe it entered alongside a physical problem like a serious illness or an emotional storm like a parental divorce. It may have arisen from something that seemed minor (a game night spent on the bench, a harsh rebuke from a parent or teacher) but left a major wound. No matter what that relationship or experience looked like, it became a door. A door for the darkness to enter your heart. A door for the shadow to slip in unnoticed. A door for Satan's lie: "You don't have a father who loves you."

Shadow of a Doubt

There was a season, though, when there were no shadows. A season before the stars were flung, before light was separated from darkness, before time was measured. A season when a bright, beautiful being roamed the heavens. A season when, some speculate, that being led the throngs in worship before the throne.

This leader, whose name *Lucifer* means *bringer or bearer of light*, became disappointed with his Father. No garage-cleaning incident marred his existence. But somehow, some way, he became convinced his Father no longer deserved his obedient service. In rage and disappointment, he made a silent vow: "I will ascend to heaven; I will raise my throne above the stars of God; I will sit on the mount of assembly in the recesses of the north. I will ascend above the heights of the clouds; I will make myself like the Most High" (Isa. 14:13-14).

When you fail to receive from your father the things you desire, you decide to take his place. You strive to fulfill the obligations you wanted him to fulfill. Lucifer's perception was wrong. Although he had a perfect Father who expressed His love and delight in everything His son did, that made no difference. The deceptive shadow moved across his heart to dull his spirit and obscure his vision. Ultimately, it led him to rebel against the most loving of Fathers.

He pursued that rebellion with everything he had. The repeated phrase: *I will...I will...I will...I will* implies emphasis. The defiant son now set his face and his heart in opposition to his Father.

Lucifer's story has no happy ending. The loving Father disciplined him. Cast suddenly out of the heavenly realm, Lucifer lost home, Father, identity, purpose, direction, destiny—he lost it all. But the shadow had already spread to the hearts of others. When he fell, Scripture says that Lucifer took one-third of the heavenly host along with him.

The shadow is dark, desperate, and greedy. Never content with its power in one life, it wants to infect and affect entire families, churches, companies, even regions or nations of the world.

Last Words

What does this have to do with you or me? In the popular words of Bruce Springsteen, "Everybody has a hungry heart." Earlier, I called this widespread problem a *shadow.* But a more specific term arises from some of Jesus' last words to His disciples. In John 14:18, he tells them, "I will not leave you as *orphans;* I will come to you."

I believe last words are important. I've been married close to forty years, and my two sons are married and living on their own. That may be why I've begun to ponder my own last words. In one of my worst nightmares, I choke out my last few breaths over a favorite snack food. Down through the generations, my descendants recall my last words: "Please pass the taco chips—ackkk, ackkk!"

This isn't the way I hope to come face to face with my Savior, and it's certainly not the way I want friends and family to remember me. I want to say something profound that will impact my descendants for generations. In view of that, I've considered the last words of some famous people:

"I die hard but am not afraid to go."—George Washington, first U.S. president

"Go away. I'm all right."—H.G. Wells, novelist

"I owe much; I have nothing. The rest I leave to the poor."—François Rabelais, writer

"It is very beautiful over there."—Thomas Alva Edison, inventor[2]

The last words we often recall are those of Christ as He hung on the cross. But another of His closing statements, spoken during the final

Supper He shared with His disciples, has intrigued me for years: "I will not leave you as orphans; I will come to you" (John 14:18).

Why would He say such a thing? Their company included business owners, a doctor, and a former tax collector. Why would Jesus speak about orphans to a group of grown men?

When I first began to study this section of Scripture, these words of the Master to His disciples made as much sense as if I said the same thing to a group of senior adults. Can you imagine the wonder in their faces if I told them, "I will not leave you as orphans"? They'd think I was crazy.

Did Jesus' followers think the same thing?

A World of Orphans

One of my main roles is that of missionary. I've spent almost forty years taking students overseas on short-term mission trips. For several years, my wife and I worked in Eastern Europe, where we served the nationals and hosted groups from the United States. We spent our summers high in the Alps conducting youth camps for the European Baptist Convention.

For the past twenty years, I've served as the president of Awe Star Ministries, a student missions-sending organization. When I'm not leading trips myself, I'm speaking about missions in churches across our country or training students to go and tell.

As a missionary, I've also done work in orphanages across the globe. As I write this chapter, I'm preparing to take a group of students to Nuevo Laredo, Mexico where we'll share the gospel through the performing arts. There, we'll also spend time with some of the many orphans we meet.

Concrete block walls and barred windows define the existence of these little ones. Their parents are either unwilling or unable to care for them, and they all know it. You can see it in the pain in their eyes and the way they cling to our students (or to anyone who offers them a kind word).

The orphanage workers tell me the hurt also shows in the way the children treat one another, the workers, and anyone else they encounter often. No matter how kind or loving the interactions, the orphans hold themselves back. The depth of their wounds makes them avoid close relationships rather than enjoy the kindness and love that comes their way.

The pain in the lives of these orphans runs deep. Closer to home, I spoke with the good people at the Missouri Baptist Children's Home. They affirmed that orphans have unique needs. "Walker," they said, "We take care of these children, we love them—and they want to hurt us. They lie. They steal little items whenever they can. They mock our value and undermine our authority. They think the whole world's against them so they must fight for their rights. No matter how much love we show them, it's never enough."

Apparently, the Mexico and the Missouri orphans are not alone. Psychologists have now identified a syndrome common among orphans. The diagnosis *Reactive Attachment Disorder* (RAD) refers to the disturbed relationships with others often exhibited by young children who have received little or no parenting.

> Children with RAD may avoid forming personal relationships. These are known as the inhibited or unattached type. On the other hand, they may seem overly friendly to everyone, not distinguishing between parents and strangers. These are known as the uninhibited or indiscriminate type. In both cases, there is no real sense of trust. The children treat other people either as threats to be avoided or as

targets to be manipulated. Not all children who are adopted internationally, the so called post-institutionalized children, are destined to have RAD. But the more emotionally and physically deprived they were, and the longer they remained in that environment, the greater their risk becomes.[3]

The Orphan Heart

Do the symptoms of RAD send a shiver down your spine, too? I ache for the orphans and adoptive families it affects. Some of these are my close friends or friends and family members of people I know. But another syndrome carries a much broader and more damaging impact: the spiritual version of RAD, something I've learned to call the Orphan Heart.

As I prayed about Jesus' promise not to leave His disciples as orphans, God brought some new teaching my way. It came from the late ministry leader Jack Frost. Like me, Jack grew up with a controlling father whom he loved but could never please. His book, *Experiencing Father's Embrace* (Destiny Image, 2006) introduces the concept of the Orphan Heart.

> I felt like such a failure, yet I wanted Dad's approval so much I kept striving to perform for him. *If only I can hit the ball right*, I told myself, *Dad will be proud of me*. I did not realize that an ungodly belief (stronghold) was growing stronger and stronger in me. I was slowly being consumed by a deep fear of failure and rejection, a fear that caused me to feel worthless unless I performed well enough to win my father's approval.[4]

Jack grew up to become a top commercial fishing boat captain, someone who had to do and be the best no matter the cost. When he came to know Christ in his late twenties, he experienced joy for the first time. The burden of sin and overwhelming addiction lifted and he began to serve God. Eventually, he became a pastor and ministry leader.

But something was missing. Jack continued to live as a driven man. His ministry was a veneer that hid his intense competition with anyone he viewed as more blessed or more gifted than he. Although his family experienced his angry outbursts, in the public arena he became a master of disguise. He hid his selfishness, his hatred, and his envy of others' success.

The difference between the public and the private Jack eventually led both of his children to close their hearts and spirits to his input. His wife, outwardly loyal, experienced inward depression and oppression. And Jack himself? You guessed it. He was miserable. He knew he was living a horrible, painful lie.

How did he escape this cycle of hatred? His book explains that freedom came only through God's intervention. Jack and his wife attended a conference on emotional healing so she could receive the help he believed she needed. Suddenly, a platform speaker asked God to give His love to any men present—to provide the love their fathers had been unable to give. Immediately, his heavenly Father's presence, compassion, and acceptance fell upon Jack as an overwhelming flood.

That prayer and experience changed Jack Frost's life. He finally understood the lie that drove his actions and responses. He'd sought the love of his earthly father when all along he had access to a much deeper, much more powerful love. His Father loved him. He mattered to God.

Common Need, Uncommon Love

The boy who spent all day cleaning his father's shop. The orphans who can't form healthy relationships because of their deep father-wounds. The fishing captain/pastor compelled to perform out of a desire to please an impossible-to-please dad. The twelve disciples who sat around a Passover table. What do they have in common?

As I also reflected on the prayer that changed Jack's life, it all came together. *Each one needed to know the love of a Father.* You see, those orphans in Missouri—and in Mexico, and anywhere else—know they live in an institution for a reason. They have no home because they have no father. Without a father, they have no identity, no significance. They spend their days in search of who they are.

The real or imagined rejection from their fathers has left them relationally handicapped. They live their lives in constant search of love, yet find themselves unable to love God or others as they should. Despite their self-protective masks, deep down inside, they know. Something's missing, and they'll do almost anything, go almost anywhere in an effort to find it.

Deep down inside, Satan knew. He knew what he'd lost. He saw what he became. His bid to take his Father's place failed, so he set about opposing Him in as many ways as he could. Scripture calls Satan the "father of lies" (John 8:44). And what better way for him to oppose a Father whose name is truth (John 14:6)?

The only way an orphan can feel good about himself is to bring others into an orphan state, too. And that statement captures Satan's evil intent.

God loves you so much that He sent His only Son to die for you (John 3:16). He longs to bring you into a father-child relationship. You matter to God. So how does our enemy counteract this truth? By doing his best to spread the biggest lie, one that produces more and more orphans. It comes in many forms, all with a similar sound and an identical effect: *You don't matter. You don't have a father who loves you. You're a loser. Your ideas are stupid.* And *Nobody cares about you.*

A Tale of Two Orphans

One of Christ's most famous parables concerns two brothers. Like many brothers, these two were complete opposites. The older brother was capable, responsible, and self-reliant. His father could count on him to get a job done and get it done right. He showed up when you needed him and when you didn't. He took his responsibilities seriously. He took *life* seriously.

The younger brother, however, didn't take much of anything seriously. You know his type. He'd take a wild idea and run. His philosophy: "It's easier to ask forgiveness than to ask permission." The younger brother, like many younger brothers, was the center of attention, the life of the party, and (as his brother saw things) a spoiled brat.

One day, the younger brother needed some cash. Instead of requesting a few shekels, he went for it all. He demanded his inheritance early by thirty years or so. This was a blow not only to his father, but to Jewish custom as well. Nonetheless, the father, as fathers often do, granted his son's request.

Maybe you know the story. Maybe you've lived it yourself. The son took the money and ran as far away as he could. Determined not to follow in his father's footsteps, he drank, he partied, and he chased wild women. He even did what no good Jewish boy should ever do: he lived high on the hog.

But do you know the flip side? The older brother stayed home. He didn't ask for his inheritance. He didn't ask for anything, at least not right away. He plowed the fields. He took care of the herds. He did it all. He may have muttered under his breath about his spoiled younger brother, but he kept working as though his life depended on it. And in his mind, it did.

And then came a sudden turn of events. The younger brother went from high on the hog to the bottom of the pork barrel. Desperate, he took a job with the worst possible employer for a young Jewish boy: a Gentile pig farmer.

Mud, muck, and manure make great eye-openers. *What a life! Dad's poorest slaves have it better than I do. I get it. I'll go home and throw myself on his mercy. If I can't be a son, I'll be a slave. But I'm going home. Home to my father.*

Meanwhile, back at the kosher ranch, Dad was waiting, watching, and praying. We know this because Scripture tells us he saw his son "while he was still a long way off" (Luke 15:20b). The father ran to his son, embraced him, and ordered his servants to prepare a celebration. Party time!

Party time, that was, for everyone except the older brother. Out sweating in the field, he heard the reverberating thump of the drums, the rhythmic pounding of feet. He finished his final chores and hurried up to the main tent to see what was happening. *Did I forget Mom's birthday? Or maybe—did Dad finally decide to reward me for all that extra work?*

What? He rubbed his eyes. *Surely not. Dad would never—but wait. It is him! That little twerp's come running home to Daddy. And now, just look at him. He's got Dad's ring. They've killed the calf I was saving for the temple potluck, and they didn't even invite me.*

Just wait. I've got something to say about this. Just wait.

His father's response matched his godly character. He spoke as gently as he could to his disgruntled older son, but he couldn't stop his celebration of the younger. He viewed both his boys through eyes of love and compassion. He saw their highs and lows, their successes and failures. And he did what God created fathers to do: he loved them.

The Rest of the Story

Although both brothers had a father, they lived as orphans. Somehow, sometime, a shadow had crept across their hearts. The younger brother responded as a rebel who turned his back on his dad. If Dad said it was black, he knew it was white. If Dad wanted him to try it, he made sure to avoid it. The crux of his rebellion came when he snatched his inheritance and got out of town. The shadow of the Orphan Heart convinced him to make the choice: *I'll take care of myself—by myself.* With that one dark decision, he moved himself from life as a son to the life—the desperate, broken, unlovely life—of a slave. *SLAVE TO SIN*

But do you see that the older brother had an Orphan Heart, too? Although he never left the father physically, he'd made his emotional departure long before. He poured out all his labor, all his obedience, all his time in an effort to prove to his father that he was good enough, smart enough, and nice enough to be treated as a son. And in the process, he made himself a slave.

The common element that ties these two different types of orphans together is the key God showed me. It's the common element between the orphan Walker Moore and the orphans who come from Russia or inner-city Nuevo Laredo. The common element is the biggest lie: the lie that says your father doesn't love you. This lie says you don't matter, that you deserve to live as a slave rather than a beloved family member.

The Orphan Heart affects us all in different ways because we're different types of people. Some end up like the younger son. We grab all we can. We take things by force because we can't trust anyone else. Others end up like the older brother. We give and serve others on the outside but remain bitter, angry, and explosive within.

In spite of their actions and responses, both brothers had a father who loved them. Because they bought into the biggest lie, they both made wrong choices. They didn't have to live as orphans, but both of them did just that.

Because I bought into the same lie, I spent many years living an orphan lifestyle. Until I understood the depth, breadth, and length of the Father's love, I believed I had to prove myself in every circumstance. Like the older brother, my perfect exterior hid an angry, bitter interior.

So what happened to change me? No, my earthly dad didn't throw me a big party (although he did other things that showed his love). But he never wrapped his arms around me or announced to others how proud he was of his beloved son.

So how did I grow to understand a love deeper than anything my father could give? How did I learn to escape the lie? How can you? If "everybody's got a hungry heart," how can you escape it? How do you learn to embrace true freedom from the Orphan Heart and its effects? How can you learn the truth that says you have a Father who loves you—and then live as though you believe it?

We'll spend the rest of this book exploring the answers to those questions. I pray you'll join me in the journey: a journey away from the Orphan Heart and into the truth that will set you free. A journey that prepares you to love others in the way God intended all along. A journey that says you matter to God, and you matter to others, too.

Author's Note: At the end of each chapter, you'll find an interactive feature called "The Battle." Escaping the lie involves spiritual warfare, and these tools and suggestions coordinate with the teaching of each chapter to help you in your journey to freedom from the Orphan Heart. Please take time to read, process, and participate in each one.

The Battle: Ask God to free your heart from negative memories of your father or other authority figures. If this is an area of special struggle, you may wish to consult a Christian counselor.

2—Spiritual Anatomy:

There's got to be more than this.

"How come when men look in their hearts they don't discover something valiant and dangerous, but instead find anger, lust, and fear? Most of the time, I feel more fearful than I do fierce. Why is that? It was one hundred and fifty years ago that Thoreau wrote, "The mass of men lead lives of quiet desperation," and it seems nothing has changed. As the line from *Braveheart* has it, 'All men die, few men ever really live.' And so most women lead lives of quiet resignation, having given up on their hope for a true man."—John Eldredge, *Wild at Heart*[1]

Matt's Story, Part 1

I looked forward to this trip. Although I'd gone on a few mission trips, I'd never been to Africa. I was excited for the opportunity to go with my friend Chad and get to know him better.

I felt like I was spiritually prepared. Whenever you leave on something like that and you're a pastor, you feel like you've spent the proper time in prayer. Because you're doing the Lord's work, you feel like you're spiritually prepared for the challenges.

When we landed in Chicago, everything was good. But the moment we got on the plane from Chicago to Doha, Qatar, it was like the darkness hit me right in the face. It was a huge plane, and as I turned to head down the aisle, I had all sorts of negative thoughts: Where do you think you're going? Who do you think you are?

I texted my wife, asking her to pray for me. I felt very anxious and claustrophobic; I knew none of this was from God.

As I sat in the seat waiting to take off, I remember thinking, Okay, if you're going to leave, you'd better do it now. *I had my way out all planned, but the Lord in His grace got me through.*

The enemy used the five senses to get to me. He used my eyes to see Buddhists, Hindus, and Muslims by their dress. He used the smell of different cultures to strike fear into my heart. Since we were on Qatar Airlines, they served meals based on the Islamic food regimen, and that added more fear.

By the time we landed in Ethiopia, I was a mess. It was about 1:45 a.m., and in Ethiopia, they don't let anyone come into the airport to meet you. So we went out to the parking lot, and we were basically the only two white people there. I'm not used to being the minority, and it freaked me out. True hatred began to build up in my heart. I thought, I've got to be on guard; these people are out to get me. *Finally, the gentleman showed up to take us to the place we were staying.*

We slept most of that day, but the next day, we went outside. We were staying in a little village where the school is, and we saw the kids on their lunch break. Over there, just by being white, you can quickly draw a crowd. The kids were all saying things like, "Let me show you my room," and I was telling them, "No, no." There were maybe forty-five or fifty fourth-graders all pushing me and I just got freaked out. I told them, "OK, OK, no more!" A teacher snapped his fingers, and the kids dispersed. It was like the enemy knew just how to get my anxiety going again, even by using children.

The next day we woke up and went to see some church leaders. On the way there, the enemy again used my senses to strike fear into my heart. The traffic was horrendous and the smog was horrible. I was just a nervous wreck. I struggled in the meeting with two men from Ethiopia. But ten minutes into the meeting, Chad said, "We need to pray." He prayed that God would rest in this place, calm our hearts, and focus our minds. How amazing is our Lord, that I haven't voiced one thing to Chad, but he prayed exactly according to my need. (to be continued)

As we explore the Orphan Heart, one of the first things we need to understand has to do with our creation. We need to know not just *why* but *how* we were created. Knowing why we were created helps us recognize our areas of struggle and brings about the truth in our lives. Understanding how we were created—how the Creator designed us—helps bring us into a place of true freedom.

Genesis 1:27 tells us we were made "in the image of God," who is Father, Son, and Holy Spirit, a three-in-one creation. As His image-bearers, we also carry this three-in-one element. So who are we?

1 Thessalonians 5:23 gives us a brief lesson in the anatomy of a believer. In this verse, Paul prays that our "spirit and soul and body be preserved complete, without blame at the coming of our Lord Jesus Christ." A similar description appears later in the New Testament: "For the word of God is living and active and sharper than any two-edged sword, and piercing as far as the division of soul and spirit" (Heb. 4:12a). Let's examine the various components of body, soul, and spirit so we can understand the roles they play in the Orphan Heart.

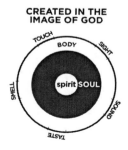

CREATED IN THE IMAGE OF GOD

Body Language

Each of us has a body, the physical door to everything that goes in our lives. In fact, the body is the door to the soul, or inner self. The avenues within the body that lead to the soul are the five senses: sight, sound, smell, touch, and taste. We experience these as the functions of the eyes, ears, nose, skin, and mouth.

In order to invade our lives with his lies and other schemes, Satan must access one of these five areas. That's why Scripture speaks so firmly about the believer's need to "crucify the flesh" (Gal. 2:20, 5:24). Apart from the sensory avenues provided by the flesh, the enemy has no way of reaching us. We'll learn more about these avenues in the next chapter. But for now, understand that he's an expert at using these five physical avenues to implant his evil messages into our lives.

A number of years ago, I attended an important meeting. One of the meeting's leaders walked in late. As soon as he saw me, he yelled, "You're shallow!" And as if that weren't damaging enough, he screamed again: "You're shallow! You're shallow!"

Thanks for the Memories?

His words penetrated my ears, echoing inside my head. My sense of hearing activated and carried them to my thought processes. Next, my brain translated the words and brought up into the forefront of my memory all the negative words I heard as a child: "You don't ever...," "Why can't you ever...?" Right there, my brain accessed a lifetime of hearing those same words repeated in various ways.

The single phrase, "You're shallow!" brought up all sorts of negative feeling and thoughts: *I'm not worthy. I have no value. I can't do anything right.* From there, other destructive comments made years earlier returned and dominated my thoughts, carrying as much pain as the first day I heard them.

How could this happen? How could such a simple statement wreak such havoc with my mind and emotions? The problem lay not with the words themselves but with the evil one's use of my senses.

Early in our lives, Satan uses the avenues of the five senses to reset our thinking. Many of the problems you experience today have to do with something said or done long ago that you received through one of your five senses. When something similar triggers that sense once again, you respond not only to what just happened, but to the long-ago input that traveled along the same sensory pathway.

I'm not sure why it happens this way, but spoken words seem to have an especially powerful effect on women. A man can say to a woman, "I like your hair," and she'll walk away, upset. Her thoughts go something like this: *He never said that before. He must not have liked it all the other days. I guess it's time to get a new hairstyle. I wonder what he doesn't like?*

At some point in the past, someone spoke unkind words to this woman about her appearance. Because of the enemy's interference with the memory, activated by the sense of hearing, even positive words related to her appearance now become a negative. This dependence on the sense of hearing may also explain why gossip seems to be a consistent problem among women. The enemy works through the avenue of hearing to twist the communication God intended for good and use it for evil instead.

On the other hand, you may not be surprised to learn that the #1 way the enemy enters the lives of men is through the sense of sight. A young boy finds his father's stash of pornographic magazines, and the images are burned into his memory forever. But a girl glances at a photo of a young man in a swimsuit, squints her eyes, and wrinkles her forehead: "Ewww, gross!"

That's why magazines like *Playboy* sell millions of copies, while *Playgirl* went out of business. Of course, porn can reach women, too, but males process visual sexual clues differently than females.[2] Because of their potentially devastating complications, we need to understand not only the avenues through which the enemy's lies reach our lives but what to do when they arrive.

Of course, not every memory has a bad or evil association. The smell of baking bread always brings my grandmother's house to mind. Grandma Moore made the best homemade bread in the world. A hungry boy couldn't find anything better than a thick, melt-in-your mouth slice of Grandma's bread, dripping with butter. Many years after her passing, I still smile when I catch a whiff of homemade bread, because I've attached to it the memories of my loving grandmother.

In the same way, realtors often tell their clients to make sure their homes not only look but smell good before an Open House. A few spices simmering in a pot on the stove, a scented candle, or a fresh-baked batch of cookies can bring up warm memories attached to positive feelings in the prospective buyers' minds. And guess what? More often than not, those positive feelings end in a sale.[3]

Retail stores spend money to pump certain scents into their stores for a similar effect. (Can you say, "Cinnabon®?") The associations people make between a particular smell and a memory from their past can affect their behavior and choices today.

So what holds the power? It's not the bread, the candle, the spices, or any other scent, but the memories we associate with them. But the enemy wants to take any memories we relate to our senses and twist them to be contrary to the Word and the will of God.

The day the man yelled at me during the meeting, I didn't remember I was a grown man with an honorary doctorate from a respected institution. I didn't remember the graduate school classes I've taught, the books and articles I've written, or the fact that I've preached to tens of thousands of people across the world. I didn't remember that even without any of these credentials, I have immeasurable worth and value.

Instead, the man's unkind words touched a memory and transported me back to a younger age. As soon as I heard what he said, my thoughts ran: *Sure, there are lots of people in the room who are smarter than I am. So many of them are wiser, with much more life experience.*

You see, every lie is a half-truth. And the more I played the comparison game, the more I agreed with my critic: *I guess I really am shallow.* I was allowing my memories and the feelings I associated with them to determine my thoughts and beliefs. Unless I take what comes in through my body via the five senses and apply the Word of God to it, I have nothing to counteract the lies of the devil.

We'll discuss this battle plan in more detail later, but unless you place God's truth against the untruths the enemy sends your way, all you can do is agree with the lies. God's Word, as Paul tells us in Ephesians 6:17, is a powerful sword. And the enemy will do his best to keep you from wielding it. He wants you to remain lost in your negative memories and trapped in his lies. But once you know and embrace the truth, it will set you free (John 10:10).

A SPIRIT-CONTROLLED LIFE

Soul Surfer

According to Scripture, our bodies have a direct connection to our souls. Near the beginning of the Bible, we learn that when God formed man and breathed the breath of life into him, "he became a living soul" (Gen. 2:7, KJV).

Again, as we learned earlier, our spiritual anatomy is broken down into body, soul, and spirit. I like the way pastor and Bible teacher Bob Smith describes the distinctions between the last two:

> Without wanting to be arbitrary, but still endeavoring to make a distinction between soul and spirit, I find the following definitions to be helpful, even though, admittedly, there seem to be areas in which soul and spirit blend and/or overlap. This is particularly true when we observe that our mind, emotions, and will function both in the realm of the spirit and of the soul. If we keep in mind the fact that there always remains an element of mystery about these distinctions, seeking to define soul and spirit still has practical value. So this is what I've settled on: The soul is the realm of *self-consciousness* and is composed of *mind*, emotions, and

will. The spirit is the realm of *God-consciousness*. The spirit of man is designed to be the place where God lives and reigns.[4]   *THE SPIRIT OF GOD IN ME.*

According to Smith, the soul has three components: emotions (what you feel), mind (what you think), and will (what you choose). The body's five senses work with the soul to help process information and determine our actions and responses.

Once we belong to Christ, Satan can't have our souls, so he looks for avenues of deceit to keep us from living the lives God wants us to have. Of the soul's three components, the emotions form the most ready path for the enemy's lies. Because our emotions are in constant flux, unless we use the Word of God tempered by the Spirit of God to balance them, they can rule our lives. Not only do our emotions change rapidly, but they also tend to have a quick trigger. They often fire off in response to something we take in through the five senses before our mind has a chance to respond in a more appropriate way.

Have you ever honked your horn when someone cut you off in traffic? That action represented an emotional response to the physical stimulus of sight. You watched the other car go where it shouldn't, and instead of thinking, "The driver must be confused" or "I bet he doesn't know where to turn," your emotions led you to push your horn hard and loud.

Although this kind of rude response may annoy your fellow drivers, it's not usually dangerous. But, as a life pattern, responding with emotions rather than sound thinking can endanger you and those around you. The parent who reacts to a child's defiant "No!" with a slap across the face; the boss who bellows, "You're fired!" when an employee makes a mistake; or the spouse who uses his fists instead of words to settle a conflict are all dangerous people who create toxic relationships.

Yes, our emotions can control us. But those who truly want to follow Christ won't allow their feelings to take such a prominent place in their lives. The proper use of emotions is to place them under the control of the will and the Word of God. And one of the main ways to do that is by accessing another component of the soul: the mind.

The mind is our organ of thought. Through the mind, we are "equipped to *know, think, imagine, remember,* and *understand.* Man's *intellect, reasoning, wisdom,* and *cleverness* all pertain to the mind."[5]

A properly-trained mind can speak to the emotions as well as the will. Proverbs tells us, "For as he thinks within himself, so he is" (Prov. 23:7). The New Testament admonishes us, "For the mind set on the flesh is death, but the mind set on the Spirit is life and peace" (Rom. 8:6) while it also encourages, "But we have the mind of Christ" (1 Cor. 2:16).

As we've seen, when our emotions get together with our mind, we have the potential to make the wrong decision. Our emotions can persuade our mind, or our mind can persuade our emotions. Or we can make an even better choice and allow the Word of God to persuade them both.

Where There's a Will

Early on in our lives, thoughts come to our minds that are contrary to the Word and the will of God. Because I grew up as a special education student who had a speech impediment and struggled in school, I had lots of negative emotions and memories that lowered my self-esteem. Years later, when the man yelled, "You're shallow!" I heard "You're stupid!," "You can't learn!," and all the other negative words hurled at me during my growing-up years.

What he said to me was unkind. But apart from the Word of God, what my thoughts and emotions whispered was crippling.

When you choose to turn your mind and emotions the right way, you can do the right thing. And this is where we see the soul's third component, the will. The will is the place of battle, where we choose or fail to choose what is right. Your will is the outward communication of the soul's choice.

I like to call the will the war zone. Here, the earthly or fleshly side and the godly or biblical side oppose one another. The side that will win is the side you feed or encourage more. If you constantly give in to selfish desires, your soul becomes trained in ungodly ways. Walk down enough wrong paths and the ruts in your soul-road will become so deep that you'll have a hard time choosing the right one.

So how do we win this war? We must train our soul according to the Word and will of God. The only way the will has the power to choose what is right, the only way it can win over the powerful emotions or the wrong thoughts implanted by the enemy, is if we take time to study and apply God's Word to our lives.

To Catch a Thief

Several years ago, I faced an important choice. Awe Star had planned to send a team to Uganda, but the political climate caused us to change our plans. Uganda revoked our visas, so we couldn't get into the country. We decided to send the team to The Gambia (another African country) instead. And that's when things got complicated.

The American airline we were using agreed to refund our ticket money but said we might not get it right away. And since only two weeks remained until the flight, the African airline refused to refund even a portion of the ticket price (close to $20,000 for that portion alone). Of course, we needed the money to buy another set of tickets so we could get our team to and from The Gambia.

Eventually, we learned that the ticket refund from the American company had gone to our travel agency. But when I called about applying the funds to our new ticket purchase, "We have a problem," the office representative told me. Our agent had embezzled our $30,000 and disappeared. No one at his office could get in touch with him, and he wouldn't answer his cell phone.

This man was a brother in Christ. I'd visited his place of business and we'd done mission work together. I couldn't understand what was happening, but I didn't know what to do about the money he had stolen, either.

"Sue him," the Awe Star Board of Trustees said.

"But he's a fellow believer. Scripture says I can't do that," I told them.

"You're not suing a brother; you're suing a business. A business isn't a believer," one of the Board members explained.

Still, I didn't have peace about the decision. I needed the money, but I just couldn't sue my brother in Christ. I asked the Board to release the decision to me, and one by one, all the members agreed. I could use money our ministry had in savings to buy the tickets, but by the end of the summer, we might be broke.

I bought the tickets anyway. I also called the travel agent and, this time, left a message on his cell phone: "I forgive you all of the debt. Your testimony is more important to me than our financial situation. A man without a testimony is a man with nothing." I called every couple of weeks to repeat the same message of love and forgiveness. But I still didn't know how we were going to cover our expenses.

Finally, he answered his phone, and I shared the same words. He seemed distressed, almost unable to respond. But I remembered God's Word says to "pray for those who spitefully use you," (Matt. 5:44, NKJV), so I continued to hold him up in prayer.

The same week I connected with him, the woman who owned the building where we had our office came in. "Walker, I need to talk to you," Becky said. My heart sank. Was she about to evict us? I didn't think I could handle one more disappointment.

"I'm selling the building," she told me. "I'm getting up in years, and I don't want to hassle with taking care of buildings anymore. I need to start selling the properties we own, especially since Claude [her husband] is gone now."

"Oh, I hope you find somebody who loves the Lord," I told her.

"I'm going to sell it to you."

What? I've just lost all this money. In three months, I won't be in business. Why would I want to buy a building? I didn't know what to say to someone who had been so kind to us.

"Becky, we don't have a building fund."

"Well, how much will you give me for it?"

Because of having to pay for insurance, I knew the approximate worth of the building—at least half a million dollars. But I didn't want to hurt her feelings, either.

"I'll give you $150,000."

"Sold."

But I don't have $150,000. I barely had the money for the plane tickets. What had I just said?

"Oh, I forgot to tell you the rest of it. I've been collecting the last five years' rent as your down payment. I already own the building, so there's no use bringing the bankers in. I can carry the note, and your next rent check is a mortgage payment."

"But what about the other renter?" At the time, another business rented space from her in the other side of our building.

"That's your problem."

So in one simple transaction, we had reduced our expenses by $12,000 a year and were now collecting rent from others. In one day, we gained $350,000 in equity. And about three months later, I went out to the mailbox and found an envelope from our embezzling travel agent with a check for $30,000 inside. He paid back everything he owed. And God had already multiplied it to make it more.

This situation had my mind, will, and emotions in a tangle. But once I applied the truth of God's Word to it, I knew what to do. Even though it may not have made sense on the outside, I knew the peace that passes understanding on the inside. Once again, God proved faithful to one whose heart was turned toward Him.

In order to win the spiritual battles we face and come out on the side of right, we need to understand a third major element of our spiritual anatomy. So far, we've looked at the body and the soul (which includes the mind, will, and emotions). But without the third critical element, we have no hope for change. And the third element is what sets Christ-followers apart. This third element is a spirit transformed by God's Holy Spirit.

**5 DOORS
TO YOUR SOUL**

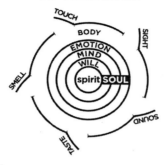

That's the Spirit!

Capitalization is a funny thing. As a schoolboy, it's something I didn't understand very well. Somewhere along the way, a teacher said to capitalize important words, so my sentences had capitals running all through them every time I thought a word was important. And when email first began, I used to write everything in capital letters. I found it easier to read that way.

One day, a friend responded to an email I'd sent. "WHY ARE YOU YELLING AT ME?" he wrote. From then on, I worked harder to use appropriate punctuation. I didn't want to yell at anyone—even through email.

As I grew older, I learned more about the rules for capitalization, although I still don't get them right every time. But in this book, when I use the word Spirit with a capital S, I'm referring to the Holy Spirit, the third person of the Trinity.

When we're born, we have a spirit. It's the place deep within us where, even before we know Him, God speaks to us. C.S. Lewis described the longing he had for God even as a young boy as a search for what he called *joy*.[6] The emptiness in his spirit cried out for God's Holy Spirit. Scripture tells us, "The heavens are telling the glory of God"

(Ps. 19:1). And the place deep inside us that receives that beautiful message is the spirit.

When we come to know Christ in the moment of conversion, Scripture tells us our human spirits are wed with God's Holy Spirit (Rom. 8:1-11). Christ now lives in us. We are "sealed in Him with the Holy Spirit of promise" (Eph. 1:13b). Now, God can speak to us in an even more direct, intimate way because, through His Spirit, He lives within us. Our spirit (little *s*) is one with His Spirit (capital *S*).

Working Out Our Salvation

What most people don't understand is that salvation itself happens in sequences. When we are saved, our spirits are saved. At conversion, each of us becomes a spiritual being, with the Holy Spirit living inside us. We're no longer citizens of this world, but of heaven, our ultimate home.

But at that same moment of salvation, our bodies remain unsaved. Until the day Christ returns, we'll all face the struggles of a fallen body. Our skin wrinkles. Our muscles weaken. And our flesh, as we've already seen, travels according to previous patterns and remains a place of weakness.

However, as Paul reminds us, the day of resurrection promises new life to even our fallen bodies: "in a moment, in the twinkling of an eye, at the last trumpet; for the trumpet will sound, and the dead will be raised imperishable, and we will be changed. For this perishable must put on the imperishable, and this mortal must put on immortality" (1 Cor. 15:52-53).

In the moment of salvation, our minds also remain unsaved. But as we spend time in God's Word, our minds experience a renewal process.

When I was first saved, I had an entire lifetime of the enemy speaking into my mind things that were contrary to the Word and the will of God. My spirit was saved. My body received the promise of salvation. But I had the responsibility to apply the Scriptures to continue the process of salvation in my soul—my mind, will, and emotions. That's the message of Romans 12:1-2: "Therefore I urge you, brethren, by the mercies of God, to present your bodies a living and holy sacrifice, acceptable to God, *which is* your spiritual service of worship. And do not be conformed to this world, but be transformed by the renewing of your mind, so that you may prove what the will of God is, that which is good and acceptable and perfect."

Renewing the mind renews the emotions and the will. That's one reason Paul tells us to "work out [our] salvation with fear and trembling" (Phil. 2:12c). The Spirit of God lives within us and has the task of revealing to us the things of God (1 Cor. 2:10-13). As we continue in God's Word, our minds are renewed, and we now have a way to evaluate the thoughts and memories put into us from our earliest days.

Jesus told His followers, "If you continue in My Word, *then* you are truly disciples of Mine; and you will know the truth, and the truth will make you free" (John 8:31b-32). Continuing in God's Word is the process many people call *discipleship*, but in truth, it's the process of working out our salvation.

When I think about this process and of God's power to renew our minds, a good friend comes to mind. Don grew up in Georgia in an era where racial bigotry was the norm. His family poured into him the idea that black people were an inferior race and culture, and his life and words showed he believed it. Even after he came to know Christ, he still held to the racist ideas he had as a young child. He was a deacon and had served on the mission field, but he was sure white people should go to white churches and black people belonged in black churches. Period. No questions. No problem.

No problem, that is, until his daughter became pregnant and married the black father of her baby. At first, Don was ready to kill the man who had violated his precious daughter. But then, the Word of God began to speak to him. He started seeing that we are all equal at the cross. He began to understand that divisions between us don't matter as much as our unity in Christ. And little by little, he began to lay down his biases and love both his new son-in-law and his grandchild.

God's Word has the power to apply itself to any area of our lives through the conviction of the Holy Spirit. And God chooses when this will occur. We can do something fifty times and feel no conviction about it when suddenly on the fifty-first time, the Spirit of God rises up in us and applies the Word to our lives. I don't always understand the way God works. But I do know that the more we "Let the word of Christ richly dwell" (Col. 3:16a) in us, the more tender our souls are toward His Spirit, and the more quickly we will respond to the truths He reveals.

Fine-Tuning

The Holy Spirit has a specific role in a believer's life: to illuminate the truth. As I write this book, I'm sitting in my office here at Awe Star Ministries. Although I can't see them, hundreds, maybe thousands, of radio signals are passing through the room all around me. But I don't hear the news. I don't hear the rock music. I don't hear the hip-hop station or the long-winded talk show host. I hear none of these programs because I don't have a radio in my office. The signals are there, but I'm not tuned in. And because I don't hear the signals, I don't respond to them, either.

If I were to bring a radio into my office, however, I could tune it to a specific station and capture a specific signal. And that's how the Holy Spirit works. He tunes in to whatever God, the one who created you and knows you, has for your life. The Holy Spirit searches through the depths of God and brings to you everything you need to have a life, a life abundant.

As we'll learn in the next chapter, the enemy has a channel through which he sends signals, too. And the message he broadcasts is always the same: *You're an orphan. You don't have a Father who loves you. You don't matter.*

The Battle: The Word of God helps us work out our salvation and renew our minds. Today read Romans 8:1-17 and take time to thank God that in Him, there is no condemnation for those who are in Christ Jesus (Rom. 8:1).

3—Voiceover:
What about those voices in your head?

"'Will I always be able to see you or hear you like I do now, even if I'm back home?'

Sarayu smiled. 'Mackenzie, you can always talk to me and I will always be with you, whether you sense my presence or not.'

'I know that now, but how will I hear you?'

'You will learn to hear my thoughts in yours, Mackenzie,' she reassured him.

'Will it be clear? What if I confuse you with another voice? What if I make mistakes?'

Sarayu laughed, the sound like tumbling water, only set to music. 'Of course you will make mistakes; everybody makes mistakes, but you will begin to better recognize my voice as we continue to grow our relationship.'"—William Paul Young, *The Shack*[1]

Julie's Story

"You don't have the brains you were born with."

Dad's words pierced my soul before I could process their meaning. I understood only one thing: he was angry. Again. What had I done to upset him now?

As I grew up, that scene repeated itself countless times. Dad's rules enclosed me like tall fences laced with twisted barbwire. I could only answer the phone with his prescribed, memorized message. I couldn't ask friends to spend the night. If he was at home, I couldn't practice my flute. In the summertime, he insisted my sisters and I spend hours on chores before we played or watched television.

I grew, and the rules did, too. None of us girls could participate in after-school activities or evenings out. He wanted us safe—safe at home. That meant we spent little time with friends. After one rare outing, I arrived home fifteen minutes late. For months afterward, Dad only allowed me to go to and from school and to Sunday church services. Nowhere else.

His rules didn't bother me nearly as much as his temper. Dad often seemed angry—his voice harsh, his words cold. And for some reason, I received the brunt of his criticism.

But I don't think he meant to be unkind. Deep down, he wanted me to become the best person I could. That's why he made so many rules. That's why he scolded me so often. That's why he was careful not to praise me. He never knew how much his heavy-handed approach hurt his sensitive middle child.

I had a daughter's natural love for her daddy, but I looked forward to the times his sales management position took him out of town. I never seemed to please him. I worked hard in school and made great grades. But the highest praise Dad gave (even when I won a coveted music scholarship) was a monotone, "Good job."

His sharp comments left deeper wounds, though. "Julie cook a meal? She can't even boil water!" "You call that work? When I was your age I could run the farm!"

Eventually, the wall around my soul stretched higher than all Dad's rules combined. If nothing could reach me, nothing could wound me. Every word, every action reflected a silent declaration: no one would ever hurt me that way again.

That's what I thought. As an adult, I lived several states away and saw my parents only once or twice a year. But I lived as though Dad was looking over my shoulder. If I tried on a new dress, I'd hear his voice: "Quit admiring yourself. You look like a duck in a pond." When I pondered a family decision, I'd hear his scornful, "You're full of beans!"

I left home, but I never left my dad. Years passed before I learned the truth that set me free.

Voices in our heads—we all hear them. Or do we?

I spent twenty years in youth ministry, long enough to earn a lifetime supply of T-shirts. Students often asked me about the voices in their heads. At first, I thought of this as one more teenage problem. Teenagers, problems—they go together, don't they? And sooner or later, most of those problems show up at the youth minister's office. *Voices in their heads. Yeah, right! All they did was overdose on video games and Mountain Dew®!*

Voices in our Heads

As time went on, though, I began to wonder: *Are these kids onto something?* When I examined my own thoughts, I realized some of them didn't sound like me at all. If I looked in the mirror, they ran like this: *You've sure gained a lot of weight. And your hair—it's already turning gray!* If the senior pastor called me to his office, I heard voices all down the hallway: *Who says you're qualified to work with youth? You didn't go to seminary! What makes you think you've got something to say?*

Were these negative thoughts my own? Or was the enemy trying his best to kill my sense of self-worth, steal my joy in ministry, and destroy my identity?

The women I know tell me they hear the voices, too. Barbara sits in the church sanctuary anticipating a wonderful worship experience when an acquaintance passes by. Suddenly, a thought blasts into her mind: *Why on earth is she wearing* that? *I wouldn't be caught dead in something so tacky!*

The voices bother Jessica when she shops for clothes. *That style always makes you look fat,* or *Your sister can wear yellow, but you sure can't.*

Did Jessica choose these self-condemning thoughts? Are they her own? And what about Barbara? Does she deliberately embrace such negative, critical ideas about another person? Or is Satan doing his best to get her to think the worst of a sister in Christ? Is he trying to disrupt the unity Jesus wants His body to have?

The more I examined what my students called "voices in their heads," the more I recognized the truth: *We all have thoughts that are not our own.*

Cartoons depict this unsettling aspect of life in a poignant way. When a character struggles with a decision, a tiny demon perched on one shoulder whispers bad choices into his ear. If his victim complies, the demon rubs his hands in glee. Atop the character's other shoulder waits a smiling, haloed angel. He whispers good, upright choices as he tries to foil his rival's attacks.

The angel and the demon are equally dangerous. That's because their cartoonish identity can convince us that the concept of hearing voices or having thoughts we can't claim as our own is only a game or childish fantasy. No matter which side wins, we lose as Christ-followers when we conclude the "voices in my head" are nothing more than a joke.

If you fail to identify the voices in your head or understand their true source, you set yourself up for trouble. But if every thought you have isn't your own, then whose is it? And if you don't have a tiny angel and demon on each shoulder, whose voices keep showing up and sounding out inside your head?

Voice Above

The question arrived with near-frightening force: "But what about you?...Who do you say that I am?" (Matt. 16:15)

Can you picture it? Overeager Peter jumped up and down in his excitement to be first to give his Master the correct answer. "You are the Christ, the Son of the living God" (Matt. 16:16).

Throughout His ministry, Jesus was as quick to praise as He was to rebuke. But this time, He didn't call His #1 pupil to the front of His class. He didn't place a star sticker on Peter's Daily Disciple Chart. Instead, He affirmed this impulsive follower with a long phrase that began, "Blessed are you" and contained a promise to give him the "keys of the kingdom of heaven" (Matt. 16:17-19).

Another significant truth hid within another statement: "flesh and blood did not reveal *this* to you, but My Father who is in heaven" (Matt. 16:17). Here, Jesus praised Peter for his response. But He also identified the source of these radical thoughts and words: His Father.

That's almost a perfect description of what I call the *Voice Above.* How did Peter know the truth? I like to put it this way: if Peter had a thousand brains and thought for a thousand years, he would never have been able to answer Christ's question correctly. In fact, all the brainpower in the world could never have given him the right answer because that answer has no source in natural knowledge.

Scripture uses the term "spiritually discerned" (1 Cor. 2:14, KJV) to distinguish this kind of truth. It can't be learned but must be revealed by our Father in heaven. And it always lines up with the Word and the will of God.

Peter knew the truth because God the Father chose to reveal it by speaking from His Holy Spirit to Peter's spirit as the Voice Above. Peter's heavenly response to his Master's earthly question showed he had heard. Almost in one breath, Jesus affirmed the truth of Peter's statement and warned the other disciples not to share it.

Voice Below

If you recall Peter's impulsive nature, you also know his victory was short-lived. Only a few verses later, Jesus described for His disciples His rapidly unfolding destiny: "that he must go to Jerusalem, and suffer many things from the elders and chief priests and scribes, and be killed, and be raised up on the third day" (Matt. 16:21).

Peter pulled Jesus aside, as anxious to set Him straight as he had been to give the right answer. "God forbid *it*, Lord!" he said. "This shall never happen to you!" (Matt. 16:22)

Who implanted this thought? I doubt Peter ever considered that question. The ideas entered his mind, and the words spilled out. But Jesus knew. His response again revealed truth, along with a firm rebuke, "Get behind me, Satan! You are a stumbling block to Me; for you are not setting your mind on God's interest, but man's" (Matt. 16:23).

Was Jesus equating Peter with Satan? Of course not. Instead, He identified the source of Peter's spoken thoughts as what I call the *Voice Below*. The messages from this voice are always contrary to the Word and the will of God.

And yes, this voice comes from Satan, the father of lies. It never tells the truth. Instead, it delivers its perversions with such clever twists that they seem pure and wholesome. When we listen to the Voice Below, we start to think wrong is right and bad is good. *Wrong is right.* Or so Eve thought when the serpent tempted her to eat the fruit God had forbidden. *Wrong is right.* Or so Aaron thought when the Israelites' complaints prompted him to fashion a golden calf. *Wrong is right.* Or so we all think when we allow Satan wrongful access to our minds, wills, and emotions.

Peter thought the Voice Below sounded wonderful. The thoughts that entered his mind and spilled from his lips matched his identity as a loyal follower and protector of his Master. His outburst gave no one a reason for suspicion. No one, that is, except Jesus. The One who identified Himself as the Truth (John 14:6) recognized the lies every time.

Voice Within

Think back to our little shoulder-sitting angel and demon. From now on, we'll replace those cartoon images with the more accurate *Voice Above* and *Voice Below*. These two work against one another in an effort to influence the third voice in our heads: the *Voice Within*.

If we're aware of any influence on our thinking, it's this one. From our earliest days of self-awareness, we hear it. Before we were born, God placed it within us as part of His ancient paths.

What are these ancient paths? The prophet Jeremiah provided a brief explanation when he wrote, "Thus says the Lord, 'Stand by the ways and see and ask for the ancient paths, Where the good way is, and walk in it; And you will find rest for your souls" (Jer. 6:16).

As I studied this passage, I looked at the Hebrew term *olam*, the word translated here as *ancient*. It means *concealed, original, timeless, out of eternity*. That means an "ancient path" extends from eternity past to eternity future. When we walk in the paths God has designed for us, we find rest because we match His desires for our lives.

We see God's ancient paths in the familiar instincts of animals. How do birds know how to build nests? Why do they fly south for the winter? These and other attributes are part of God's deliberate design, His ancient paths specific to birds. Everything God created has His ancient paths implanted deep inside.

People are no exception. The Voice Within represents a key part of God's ancient path for our lives. As a missionary, I've seen evidence for this voice in cultures across the globe. For example, I've never met a person—regardless of race, religion, or family background—who believes that rape or child abuse is right. Yes, these crimes occur, but the fact that nearly every culture and country has laws to prohibit them reflects the ancient paths implanted within us. No matter whom we are or where we live, something deep inside allows us to recognize these actions as wrong.

We don't acquire this heartfelt knowledge through an anti-violence billboard or a purity campaign. This deep moral core was implanted by a loving God, and all people—whether or not they have come to know Christ—have their own Voice Within. We also call it the *conscience.*

Paul explained the way the Voice Within coincides with God's ancient paths when he wrote:

> When outsiders who have never heard of God's law follow it more or less by instinct, they confirm its truth by their obedience. They show that God's law is not something alien, imposed on us from without, but *woven into the very fabric of our creation* [emphasis mine]. There is something deep within them that echoes God's yes and no, right and wrong. (Rom. 2:14-15, *The Message*).

The Father implants the Voice Within deep inside us so that, even as an infant who threatens to cross a forbidden threshold or a toddler who acts out his first lie, we know. We are made in God's image, Genesis 1:27 says, and the conscience reflects the goodness of His creation. Although the Voice Within can't control our decisions, it lays down a basic moral foundation that helps us know right from wrong—whether or not we respond as we should.

Long Shot

An experience I had years ago reveals the conflicts met by the Voice Within. In our rural community, our lives revolved around rain. When it didn't come, we longed for it. When we had too much, we complained about it. And nearly everyone participated in the constant stream of comparisons between the total rainfall this year and last year. My dad, like most of the other farmers we knew, lived by his rain gauge. He could tell you down to a sixteenth of an inch the exact amount of rain we had last week, last month, or last year.

One Christmas, my brothers and I decided Dad needed to update his arsenal. Today's rain gauges boast digital readouts. This one, with its bright red markings and rain cloud emblazoned on one side, was state of the art for the 1950s, and Dad affirmed the wisdom of our choice. As soon as he could escape the holiday chaos, he strode down the driveway to affix his prize to a fencepost.

I had a new present to try out, too. To a young boy, the joys of a BB gun far outweigh anything a rain gauge can offer. That may have been why, as Dad stood back to admire his new toy, I aimed straight at it from the safety of our front porch.

One voice whispered, *There's no way you'll hit it. No way.*

Another seemed more urgent: *Don't do it. You know it's wrong.*

And the first—louder, more passionate: *Go ahead. You can't hit it, anyway!*

My eyes squinted as my fingers squeezed the trigger. And as the BB sped toward its mark, "No way" became "Oh, my." Dad's prized possession exploded in front of him. And a million little pieces never looked so forlorn.

The Voice Below was after me. It battled something the Father placed deep inside me: my standard for moral living, the values-driven

Voice Within. The moment I pulled the trigger, I turned away from its urgings. And as I did, the Voice Within sounded more and more like the hatred and lies of the Voice Below.

Which Voice?

How do the Three Voices gain access to our minds and spirits? Since God implants the Voice Within deep inside you, it doesn't have to find an avenue. You hear it because it exists as part of you by divine design.

Our choices and actions shape our ability to hear this voice. As time goes on, they also shape the content of the thoughts it transmits. When Paul warned his followers about false teachers, he said their "conscience" has been "seared with a hot iron" (1 Tim. 4:2, KJV).

When you violate the moral tenets God placed within you so much and so often that the Voice Within no longer warns you, you've seared your conscience. That is when the Voice Within begins to sound like the Voice Below, a scary but common situation.

Can You Hear Me Now?

Recall your spiritual anatomy. Once you come to know Christ, you gained a regenerated spirit. God has direct access to this spirit and your renewed mind via the Voice Above. The main way the Voice Above speaks is through the Word of God. Psalm 119:105 tell us that God's Word is a "lamp to [our] feet and a light to [our] path."

We receive the revealed truth of Scripture as input from the Voice Above. Jesus referred to this when He told His disciples it was to their advantage that He goes away, because the Helper would come. "He will teach you all things and bring to your remembrance all that I said to you" (John 14:26).

We also hear the Voice Above when we communicate with God in prayer or worship. That's how we can "pray without ceasing" (1 Thess.

5:17) and gain the "peace which surpasses all understanding" (Phil. 4:7 NKJV). Scripture contains many examples of times when God's people waited before Him and heard His voice, as young Samuel listened in the temple (1 Samuel 3) or as the young shepherd David worshiped in the field.

God speaks to believers through His people, too. In the New Testament era, *fellowship* between believers meant time and conversation focused on the things of God—not food, as we so often think today. Your heavenly Father may choose another believer to speak into your life. He did this when He sent the prophet Nathan to confront David. And He has done it for me countless times through the wise counsel of my wife and ministry partners.

It can be tough to listen when God speaks through someone you know, especially if it's something you don't want to hear. But ask Him to open your ears. The depth of His love means He has your best interests at heart.

Speak Out

The Voice Above has two more ways to reach us. Both involve the situations God brings into our lives. Sometimes the Voice Above communicates through circumstances that show us God's work and ways. Perhaps we receive a job offer or encounter someone we didn't expect to see. Although we should never elevate experiences to replace the Word of God, it seems clear that He can orchestrate situations in a way that allows the Voice Above to reach us.

This happened to me not long ago when I tried to arrange transportation for a church mission team in the Ivory Coast. I arrived in a city where I didn't know the language and had few contacts. All previous attempts to secure vehicles had failed. The church couldn't afford the

$1000 per day the rental agents demanded. But how else could the team travel to remote villages to share the gospel?

God spoke through circumstances when He allowed me to meet with a group of overworked pastors. As we spent time together, I shared our team's need. I ended up renting two brand-new Mercedes vans from one man's church for only $100 apiece per day. God spoke as clearly through those circumstances as if He had sent me an email or written on my office wall.

One final set of circumstances transmits the Voice Above more clearly than almost any other. God uses the vehicle of suffering to silence other voices and allow us to hear from Him.

I learned this through one of the most painful seasons of my life. As a young youth pastor, I moved from a large church in Dallas to a smaller church in north Texas. This town sits sixty miles past the great Commission. You drive to the ends of the earth, turn left, drive sixty more miles, and you've arrived. But the town's location seemed minor compared to the things our family faced there.

As soon as we arrived in our new town and church, virtually everything we touched turned to Texas-sized dust. Instead of watching the youth ministry expand, we saw young people stay away in droves. Next, our only vehicle failed, and we had no savings to replace it.

We could have turned to each another for support. Instead, my wife and I had problems—serious problems. I sank into deep depression. Every night when I returned from the church, I went straight to bed. The day came when I was at the end of my resources and nearly at the end of my rope. I lay on the drab green carpet of my office, pulling out soiled tufts as I screamed out, "I hate you, God! I hate you! You've taken everything away!"

In that awful moment, I heard God more clearly than I'd ever heard Him before. The Voice Above reached into my suffering and said, "I thought I was everything to you. I'm the Alpha, the Omega, and everything else in between."

For the first time in my life, I got it. I realized that if I put my happiness on anything besides Jesus, I would lose. My lesson? Jesus plus nothing equals everything or, as I like to put it, J + 0 = E.

The Voice Above spoke through my suffering to reveal a truth that transformed my life, my marriage, and my ministry. When God speaks through suffering, we listen. At that point, we have nowhere else to turn.

Purpose-Driven Death

The Voice Above reaches us through several avenues. But what about the Voice Below? We need to understand that the voices in our heads are not always our own. But we must also learn to recognize how and why they approach us. This is especially true in the case of the Voice Below. If we can recognize its goals and its approach, we have the opportunity to stop it before it utters a single deadly word.

The good news is that the Voice Below uses only one main avenue. It longs to put into our lives everything contrary to the Word and the will of God. To do so, it makes its entrance through our physical body or as Scripture puts it, our *flesh*. When we come to know Christ as Savior, Satan can do nothing to destroy or remove that relationship (John 10:27-29). So he does the next best thing: he speaks to our flesh as the Voice Below. He wants to make us think and act as though we have no salvation and no relationship with the Savior.

John 10:10 sets forth the contrasting goals of the Voice Below and Voice Above: "The thief comes only to steal and kill and destroy; I came that they may have life, and have *it* abundantly." Since every perfect gift comes from above (James 1:17), it makes sense that the enemy wants to take away those gifts.

The whispered words of the Voice Below can convince believers to substitute God's love with carnal love. It tells us to trade God's peace for false peace from drugs or other addictions. The Voice Below steals by causing us to exchange God's truth for the enemy's horrible lies. *Go ahead—you deserve it. And it'll make you feel so much better!*

One of the most devastating lies the Voice Below whispers is the one that says your life has no importance. You're at the wheel of your car when suddenly the thought strikes you: *What would happen if I pulled out in front of that truck?* This and every thought of suicide comes from the Voice Below.

Satan does not have power over life and death. That power belongs to God alone. But the Voice Below will do anything to convince us life isn't worth living. It does its best to fill an individual's mind with thoughts of hopelessness, worthlessness, and despair. After all, the enemy's darkest, dearest hope is to convince someone to take his own life.

Satan's final goal is to destroy our impact on eternity. Here, the whispered lies of the Voice Below convince the believer to live like the world. *You're forgiven, so it doesn't matter what you do. God has to accept you in heaven, so you may as well live the way you want right now.*

Breaking and Entering

As we learned in the last chapter, the Voice Below can only gain access to us through one door: the physical body, the flesh. But if the flesh is the door, the five senses are the hallways that lead there. Sound, sight, touch, smell, and taste are all avenues that allow it to penetrate and whisper its lies.

Remember the childhood song, "O Be Careful, Little Eyes"? We must make sure our eyes are careful because our bodies haven't yet been made holy. Because of the Fall, our flesh leans toward choices that pull us away from God's divine design. As Scripture teaches, these wrong desires "wage war against your soul" (1 Pet. 2:11).

What does this mean in practical terms? Think about the five senses. God designed and intended them only for good. But when the Voice Below uses the senses, *good* becomes *evil*. Sight, taste, touch, and smell are used for some of the most horrible forms of physical or sexual perversion. And the amazing gift of hearing allows the spoken words of others (like Julie's dad in the story that opens this chapter) to penetrate deep into our minds and spirits. That's when the Voice Below sounds like the voice of a parent, a sibling, or another who taunted, teased, or otherwise hurt you.

Think back to your childhood. Perhaps you had a brother or sister who made fun of your appearance. Or maybe it was the kids at school. Way back then, the Voice Below whispered, "You're ugly," through the mouths of many people. Each time you heard it, the idea *You're ugly* became less an outer insult and more a part of your inner identity. The Voice Below was out to get you—and it did.

God, through the Voice Above, says you are "wonderfully made" (Ps. 139:14). You matter. But if you're not careful, the Voice Below will use your senses to make you believe the exact opposite.

The Biggest Lie

Most people walk around our world today believing a lie—a lie that says they don't matter. The Orphan Heart is the deepest and most original expression of the Voice Below. It's the one that asked Eve, *Has God really said?* It's the one that whispered to Julie, *You don't have the brains you were born with.* It's the one that causes so many of us to run from our earthly father and avoid our heavenly one. And it's the one that, left unchecked, can grow within an individual until it's indistinguishable from the Voice Within.

When we confuse the Voice Below with the Voice Above, we receive it as the Voice Within. At that point, we exchange the truth for a lie. We receive the enemy's deceptive input as our own thoughts from our own minds. At that point, we've developed what Scripture calls a *stronghold.*

The most basic, most dangerous stronghold of all is the one that pulls you away from the love of your Father and identifies you as an orphan. The biggest stronghold of all whispers the lie *You don't have a father who cares for you.* The biggest stronghold of all is the Orphan Heart.

The Battle: One of the best ways to conquer the Voice Below is to remain in His Word. During your quiet time today, underline any Bible verses that speak against the lies of the enemy. For example, "When I am afraid, I will put my trust in You" (Ps. 56:3) combats the lie of fear.

4—Identity Theft:
You don't know who you are.

No father, no identity.

"Since she had been living in other people's houses and had no Ayah, she had begun to feel lonely and to think queer thoughts which were new to her. She had begun to wonder why she had never seemed to belong to anyone even when her father and mother had been alive. Other children seemed to belong to their fathers and mothers, but she had never seemed to really be anyone's little girl."—Frances Hodgson Burnett, *The Secret Garden*[1]

Zach's Story

When I was growing up, people would annoy me with the constant question, "Are you going to grow up and be a preacher, too?" I couldn't understand why everyone thought I had to do what my daddy did. Preaching was the last thing I wanted to do—ever.

So somewhere along my journey, maybe as early as elementary school, I started thinking about being a doctor. And the idea stuck.

Later, after I had accepted Christ during my college years as a pre-med student, I remember reading Scripture and seeing myself preaching these passages to God's people. My dad encouraged me to keep following God and He would show me what to do. So I did (or so I tried).

But God never released me. I never had peace about becoming a preacher, so I carried on with where I believed God was leading me...

After marriage, medical school, and a renewal seminar that brought great healing into my life, I was still struggling. Somehow, God began to show me I was drawing my sense of identity from others and not from Him. So I began to regularly confess that, submit myself to God in that area, and meditate on what He was saying. And one day, I finally understood why, as a young child, I had chosen medicine as my career.

A large part of my relational woundedness concerning my parents centers on the topic of respect, a vital area for a developing young man's confidence and journey to manhood. At a young age (with specific regard to my parents), I had subconscious feelings of not being respected and valued for who I was. I remember thinking how respected physicians were and that I would be respected——especially by my parents——if I were to become a physician.

Now, I realized none of this was true. I know who I am: a gentle and original man. Earlier in my life, I couldn't have become a preacher because I would have derived my identity from my occupation rather than from Him. But my identity was penned by my Father in heaven before time began. He wrote it into my DNA and used the experiences in my life to make me who I am. Christ is at the center of me and surrounds me, all at once. I don't need the MD behind my name to prove a thing.

God has been rewiring and re-teaching me about where I draw my sense of identity from. Today, I'm free of the obligation to be something or become someone in order to fulfill emotional/spiritual needs. I can acknowledge the relationships in my life for the way each of them plays an important role in making me who I am and the interplay between them. This empowers me to make better decisions because my relationships are further purified of imbalance and sin. And someday, when the time is right and the doors open, I will go into full-time ministry: preaching, writing, leading, and loving God's people.

At one time or another, most of us struggle with our identity. And many of us, like Zach, try to give ourselves an identity that may or may not fit.

When our courts examine whether legislation is appropriate, they go back to our country's original document—the Constitution—and see how it lines up with what the Founding Fathers intended. In the same way, if we want to learn about our identity, we must go back to God's original document, the Bible, and see what He says.

Smoke Detector

I don't know if you realize it, but we're in the process of tracing a smoke trail back to the fire. Jesus' statement, "I will not leave you as orphans" (John 14:18) is the smoke. But where's the fire? Or in this case, where did we lose our Father? Where did we lose our identity?

The smoke trail goes all the way back to Genesis 1, which describes the world in a state of chaos. The earth was "formless and void, and darkness was over the deep, and the Spirit of God was moving over the surface of the waters" (Gen. 1:2). Into this chaos stepped God, who spoke order into disorder.

Here, God did two things. First, He separated the day from the night, and next, He gave each one a special name: "God called the light day, and the darkness he called night" (Gen. 1:5a). Naming always brings order to disorder. From that moment forward, day and night have never gotten confused again. Until the day Christ returns, they will keep marching out the order in which God placed them.

Later in Genesis 1, Adam entered a world of beautiful confusion. When God breathed life into the man He had formed from dust, all the right elements for a lovely garden were there, but without any specific arrangement. So God charged Adam with the critical task of bringing order into the world by having him give names to all the cattle, the birds of the sky, and the beasts of the field (Gen. 2:20).

Names matter to God. When God named Adam, He gave him his identity. In the New Testament, we see this in the baptism of Jesus, when the Father pronounced His blessing over His Son: "You are My beloved Son, in You I am well-pleased" (Luke 3:22). His Father's declaration of name and blessing made Jesus' identity settled and secure.

By God's original design, then, parents have the job of speaking identity into the children of the family. But the Fall took Adam and his descendants away from that task and into the struggle for identity that defines everyone with an Orphan Heart.

When God expelled him from the garden, Adam lost his identity. Instead of walking, talking, and working in close proximity to his heavenly Father, he experienced the separation of sin. For the first time, buying into the enemy's lie put distance between the first man and God. And that distance led to a loss of identity. Adam no longer knew who he was and to whom he belonged.

Isn't that what sin does? It steals our identity. Every day, we see this played out in relationships. When the deceitfulness of sin enters a marriage, husband and wife become distant from one another, experiencing an emotional, spiritual, and often a physical separation. The longer this separation continues, the more their identity as a couple dissolves. Their identity, like their relationship, is no longer secure.

In the same way, rebellious children put distance between themselves and their parents. The further they go from family values and ideals, the less secure they are in their identity.

When a relationship is close, it is also secure. But a widening, gap, or break in relationship allows Satan to insert lies that make us doubt who and what we are. Proximity brings identity. Distance dissolves it.

The smoke trail takes us back to the garden and back to the first whispered lie—"Did your father really say?"—that marked the beginning of the Orphan Heart.

The trail of smoke leads back to the snake in the garden. When we fail to receive identity from our fathers, no matter what the reason, we spend our lives searching for it. Creation without identity yields a life of chaos. And a life of chaos is far from the Father's plan.

What's in a Name?

A friend of mine, Larry, has been involved in prison ministry for some time. On one occasion, he was locked in a federal prison for an entire weekend of ministry with Chuck Colson and Prison Fellowship. During the weekend, he had the opportunity to spend time with a man who had just received Christ.

Larry went over to talk to the man. And as he did, he decided to practice something I often do with my students on the mission field: rename them with a name that reflects not a lack of identity but the new work God has done in their lives. Larry wanted to help bring order from the disorder in this man's life.

"What's your name?" he asked the prisoner.

"Earl," came the response.

"Well, Earl, I see you as more of a Peter, the guy who preached the truth in season and out of season. I think God has a brand-new minister here in you. Would it be all right if I called you 'Peter' from now on?"

The new Peter's smile lit up the room.

Right after that, a man got up to speak—and preached an entire sermon about the apostle Peter. "He's talking about me, he's talking about me!" Larry's new friend said.

Within just a few short minutes of being renamed, this man's attitudes and actions showed a huge turnaround. God was using Larry to break the lies the enemy had spoken into him and to bring his identity back into line with the person God had known Earl was all along.

In a Fix

We can see now why men tend to be doers and fixers. During the time of creation, God spoke order into disorder and gave Adam the charge of following His example. But ever since the Fall, men no longer speak order into disorder in a positive, pleasing way. Instead, we speak into ourselves.

Have you ever heard two men right after they return from a fishing or hunting trip? They don't talk about the beautiful scenery they saw or the delicious meals they cooked over the campfire. Instead, most of the time, they speak into themselves. They brag about who caught or shot the biggest and best. They tease each other—in fun, but with a sting of truth—about any inadequacies revealed along the way. And they take turns not praising each other but finding subtle ways to speak into themselves.

This self-acclamation doesn't limit itself to outdoor activities, though. Men speak into themselves about their jobs, too. Try staying in a hotel where a medical convention is taking place. The egos can barely fit into the elevator. And I hate to say it, but the same is true for a pastor's conference. "Our church experienced tremendous growth last year," "We had over 400 baptisms in the past six months," and "We're going to have to hire new staff to keep up with all the young families who are joining" are all ways pastors speak into themselves. In effect, they're saying, "I'm bigger, I'm better, and my Sunday School teachers can beat up yours."

Men find their identities in what God created them to do: bringing order from disorder. Even if we don't have a mechanical bent, we like to solve problems, offer advice, and make it hard for anyone who only wants someone to listen without passing judgment. According to God's design, fixing is the most natural thing for us to do. And when we do it, we're demonstrating the qualities that make us most like God—our *Godness*, you might say.

But the problem is that we can't fix ourselves. No one has ever spoken our identity into us, and because of the Fall, we've lost the ability to do it. Even Adam didn't fix the chaos that entered his world after he and Eve ate the forbidden fruit. Instead, he blamed God (and Eve) for it. He should have spoken into it instead.

Children are creatures of disorder. If you don't believe that, just ask a parent. And the job of the father is to speak into that child an identity. But if you don't have identity yourself, you can't speak it into someone else.

For many years, that was my problem. I was trying to do something I couldn't. As fallen creatures, we are desperate for identity. Either our father didn't speak it into us or we believe the enemy's lies and fail to receive that identity even if he does.

As we've learned, we receive the lies when the Voice Below speaks through one or more of the five senses. He tells us we don't have a father who loves us and that we don't matter to God. And before long, like the Prodigal Son, we're heading off for foreign lands. And what do we hope to find there? Our identity—the same identity we could find waiting at home, the same identity the Father has spoken into us all along.

I like to put it this way: *No father, no identity*. Once the enemy's lies convince us we don't have a father who cares about us, we struggle to find our identity. And not having an identity, as Zach's story at the beginning of the chapter shows, can lead to all kinds of problems.

Rewired

In December, 2007, I was fulfilling a speaking engagement in the sunny warmth of northern Peru while a gigantic ice storm blew and blasted its way across Oklahoma. Every time I called my wife, she told me about more devastation. Our backyard looked like a disaster area. No, it *was* a disaster area! Huge oak, pecan, and maple tree limbs crisscrossed one another all over our lawn. Crushed under the weight of the limbs, our patio furniture lay as though King Kong had planted his foot squarely on top of it. My wife was home alone, our house had no power, and I was thousands of miles away. Family and church members came to the rescue, though, so we ended up seeing the blessing in the storm.

The electricity came back on, the furnace warmed our house, my son came and chopped up the debris, and life soon went back to normal except for one thing: our television. For some reason, the power outage messed up the small flat-screen in our living room. Oh, it worked, but the color wasn't right. After I got home, my wife asked me to fix it.

No matter how I tried to adjust the set, it wouldn't produce the color green. I opened the instruction book and studied the finer points of color correction. The *hue* button has something to do with it. I must have missed that day in art class. As I held my remote control and began to adjust the hue, the picture changed from orange to purple. When Lassie turned blue, I knew things still weren't quite right.

When I noticed the orange cows in the *National Geographic* special, I decided to go over those instructions one more time. I learned that our television has another button called *saturation*. As I adjusted this control, Lassie's coat went from royal to navy blue, and the cows changed from fluorescent orange to mauve. Again, I recognized that something wasn't quite right. This time, I noticed one more button, *color temperature*. Maybe that one would get us back on track. It did take the blue out of Lassie, but now Timmy was blue and the cows a lovely shade of pink.

For two days, I fiddled, making hundreds of adjustments. Tints, contrast, brightness, backlight—I set and reset them all in multiple combinations. Finally, I gave up and broke the news to my wife: we would either have to get this set repaired or buy another one, something we really didn't want to do with the Christmas season upon us.

As we sat on the couch discussing our bad fortune, our youngest son, who was staying with us because of the power outages in his nearby town, looked up and saw the confusion of color on the screen. "Dad," he said. "While you were gone, I hooked up my Xbox to your TV. I may not have gotten all of the wires back in the right place."

As soon as I heard this, I turned the set around. Sure enough, he had the audio plugged into one of the color slots and had reversed the color cables. Within a few minutes, I unplugged and replugged each cable into its proper place.

When I turned the television back around, guess what? Lassie was her normal color, the cows looked black and white, and the Dallas Cowboys played on the green grass in their blue-and-white uniforms. At last, the world had returned to its proper order. For the rest of the evening, Cathy and I sat watching television and admiring the beautiful picture.

As for our son, he chose that night to move back to his own home. I found myself tempted to drive over while he was at work the next day and rewire the cables on *his* television set.

As I thought about our problem, I realized that what happened to our television is exactly what the enemy does when he steals our identity. God speaks our identity into us from before we are born. Once we come to know Him, His Spirit lives within us to reassure us of our status as His beloved children.

But what does the enemy do? He rewires us. He plugs the "father" cable in where it doesn't belong, and sets the "identity" cable to receive incorrect input from evil sources. Before we know it, we're looking for our identity in our work, our appearance, our looks—anywhere but in Him. The enemy resets our affections and rewires our identity. And once this is accomplished, the colors can't come out the right way.

The reason the picture with the wrong colors bothers us is that God has imprinted the true picture on every man's heart. And that's where the disconnect of the Orphan Heart comes in. We know something's wrong, something's missing. And it troubles us when the colors come out wrong.

Who Am I?

But our identity crisis goes even farther than the individual or the family. Like many other problems, it spills over into our society as well.

Since I was born in 1951, I went to high school during the '60s. My entire generation became known for rejecting its authorities. We grew our hair long, we started communes, we took LSD, we smoked marijuana, we protested anything we didn't like (and some things we did), and we gave *Woodstock* a whole new meaning.

In all of those actions, what did we do? We rejected those who gave us our identity and went out to find it on our own. So we have an entire generation who grew up with Orphan Hearts. Today, we have masses of people wandering around and bumping into each other like pinballs in a machine, trying to find their identities.

Until we fix the problem of the Orphan Heart, we'll continue to see this problem in individuals, in families, and in entire cultures. The other day, I talked to a missionary from North Korea. He wants me to teach these principles in his country, because, as he says, "Our culture produces orphans." It seems when we don't know how to solve a problem, we make it part of our culture. That happens not just in North Korea but all over the world.

Neither the Prodigal Son nor his older brother (Luke 15) believed his father loved him. Since God designed fathers to speak into us our identity, when we don't have a father or don't receive his words, we end up in an identity crisis. We don't know who we are. And when we don't know who we are, we don't know what we do. Like Zach, who based his entire education on a lie, we go searching for ourselves in all the wrong places.

That's why we need to escape the lie of the Orphan Heart. And that's why the exploration we've done so far only touches a small part of this powerful, evil force.

5—Guilt Trip:
You can't escape your past.

No father, no identity.
No identity, no purpose.

"Guilt wears track shoes. Sprint, marathon, or cross-country; it doesn't matter. It runs tireless to catch you, and it carries a sledgehammer."—Jamie Mason, *Three Graves Full*[1]

Donnie's Story

Donnie never knew his father, not the way anyone would want to. All he could remember of his dad was a loud voice, hard boots, and a belt that would swing and slap until it raised bright purple welts on his narrow back.

His mom finally took Donnie and his sister and moved out west. But I've seen the scars from those beatings. And now, I know how deep they reached.

Donnie's the type of guy who succeeds at almost anything he tries. Speaking, sales, youth ministry—you name it, and he rose to the top.

I met him when our church called him as youth minister. Right away, everyone loved him. The youth group grew like crazy, and he even started a special fund to help any kid in the local high school go to camp.

I felt honored when he'd call me to solve a last-minute problem or run an errand. I loved to help, and when he asked me out, I couldn't believe it. Maybe God had someone for me after all.

I should have had a clue when the police called after my truck was stolen. They found it wrecked on the side of the road in another state. Guess who was behind the wheel?

When Donnie showed up at my door in tears, I didn't know what to think. "I would've asked you," he pleaded. "But I had to help my little sister leave her abusive husband. How could I say no?"

I forgave him, of course. Soon, we were engaged. But I wondered about the college fund a Sunday School class set up for him. I never saw him study or take a test. And it seemed odd that he couldn't make his rent but gave me a 3-carat diamond engagement ring.

Things came to a head after the annual youth camp fundraiser. Just as it began, Donnie rushed in, crying. "My mom! She's gone! I can't believe it!"

We all wanted to help. Right there, we collected enough to pay for his trip back to California.

We had some leftover money, so our pastor called the small-town funeral home to check on expenses. But Donnie hadn't been there that week. And no one with his mother's name had died. When the pastor checked on the youth camp fund, he figured out that more than half of the money had disappeared.

Just like Donnie. It turned out he'd cheated, lied, and stolen from almost everyone he knew. I really didn't know who this man was. And do you know what? He didn't either. He hid behind all kinds of masks. One day, the guilt and shame got to be too much, and he moved on.

I may have missed my chance at marriage, but I didn't miss out. Oh, and my 3-carat diamond ring? You guessed it. Donnie stole that right along with my heart. I turned it in to the local police.

I still feel sad, and I still pray for Donnie. With his web of lies, he wasted the gifts that could have brought glory to God. Maybe someday, the truth will set him free.

Let's take another look at our friends Adam and Eve. Do you remember what happened after they chose to eat the forbidden fruit? They experienced two powerful emotions that we're all too familiar with today: *guilt* and *shame*.

I know how they felt because I can see both guilt and shame reflected in their behavior. In the past, this first family had walked and talked with God in His beautiful garden. The three had a healthy, give-and take relationship. But once they sinned, their behavior changed. The garden no longer seemed like home. And instead of looking forward to spending time with their loving Father, they did their best to hide from Him.

Shame on You

Of course, Adam and Eve couldn't really hide from an all-knowing, all-wise Father. His words, "Where are you?" (Gen. 3:9b) don't come because He can't figure out Adam's location. He hadn't suddenly lost His child. God was using His question to make Adam realize how far he had gone, not just in his disobedience, but in attempting to hide from His Father.

Adam and Eve experienced guilt because they did the wrong thing. In eating the fruit, they disobeyed the Father's direct command. The Bible calls this *sin*. Guilt is external, our direct response to an awareness of sin. Guilt is the knowledge that we did something wrong.

But shame flows out of relationship. We experience it when our sin makes us think someone we respect disapproves of us. In that way, shame comes from our awareness of our guilt. And the result of shame, as we've already seen, is the desire to hide. Just like Adam and Eve, and just like Donnie, we hide from the one(s) we feel we've disappointed.

The reason Adam had to hide was because he couldn't look at God. He had internalized his guilt, and it became shame. Guilt is what makes you hang your head, knowing you've done something wrong. But shame keeps you from lifting your head and looking that person you respect in the eye. Guilt says, "I did something wrong." Shame says, "I'm a bad person."

Guilt leaves a mark. Shame leaves a wound that doesn't heal.

This is all part of what I call the downward spiral of the Orphan Heart: a series of lies from the enemy that lead you to believe you don't matter to God. In the last chapter, we looked at the first lie, "You don't know who you are," or, as I put it, "No father, no identity."

When we come to faith, God lives inside us as the Holy Spirit. But the enemy works to steal, kill, and destroy all the good work God wants to do in our lives. Once he convinces us that we don't have a Father who cares, he has effectively stolen our identity. He rewires our thinking so we believe the lie. And once that lie takes over, he whispers another: "You can't escape your past," or, in my shortened version, "No identity, no purpose."

When Adam and Eve ate the forbidden fruit, they experienced the true guilt that occurs when we do something wrong. God can use this guilt to move us to repent and ask forgiveness. But when we lose our identity, we no longer trust our Father. Instead of dealing with our guilt in an appropriate way, we internalize it, resulting in shame.

As we've seen, shame leads us to hide. And here's where the enemy must rub his hands in glee. When we hide, we can no longer fulfill the purpose God has for our lives. *No identity, no purpose.*

Hide Away

When Adam hid from his Father, he lost the whole purpose God had for him in the garden. Do you remember? Right before the Fall, God showed Adam that purpose: "Then the Lord God took the man and put him into the garden of Eden to cultivate it and keep it" (Gen. 2:15).

God didn't intend Adam to walk around aimlessly, following a butterfly here and smelling a flower there. Instead, God made him the caretaker for His garden. The Hebrew verb for *keep* at the end of the verse actually means "to exercise great care over."

Adam was more than just a garden ornament. He had a purpose, and that purpose made him an active participant in Eden's nurture, work, and watch-care. But after sin came into the world, what was Adam doing? Not caring for the garden. Not tending plants or pulling up the newly-sprouted weeds. Instead, he was hiding—from God, from his responsibilities, and from his purpose in life. No longer did he consider it his purpose to carry out the will of his heavenly Father. His new purpose, drawn straight from the enemy's lair, was to hide.

Notice that God didn't come to Adam and say, "Why aren't you doing your job?" He didn't slap him with angry words like, "Why aren't you taking care of My garden?" Instead, He asked the simple question "Where are you?" Adam's purpose, the very thing he was supposed to be doing, had been neglected and set aside because of his shame. And he and Eve were already becoming experts in the fine art of hiding.

Some people refer to hiding as wearing a mask. We feel guilt over the wrong things we've done. But instead of facing our guilt, we internalize it and allow shame to grow. So to cover the wounds our shame creates, we put on various masks.

Our masks can give us a happy face when we're crying inside or a confident face when we feel afraid. Our masks can make us the life of the party or the belle of the ball. Depending on how expert we are in the art of hiding, we can change our masks to fit the person we're with or the situation we encounter.

All this comes about because we, like Adam and Eve, are hiding. We can't let anyone see the real person behind the mask. We need to leave it in place to hide the deep, gaping wounds created by shame.

Instead of putting on a mask or heading for a foreign land like the Prodigal Son, Adam hid behind a convenient bush. For some people, the bush is perfection: "I'll please my father by doing everything right." For others, it's rebellion: "I won't do anything he tells me to do."

Whether you call it a mask, a bush, or a foreign land, when you look behind it, you find a broken person. Shame ties us to the past and to the guilt of our sin. It prevents us from moving into the purpose God has for our lives. And that's why the enemy works, as he did with Adam and Eve, to move the guilt of your sin into enduring shame.

Guilty as Charged

However, we can feel guilt without it ending in shame. I hate to say it, but I'm a good example of that right now.

Whenever I fly, I can always tell when the plane is getting close to Tulsa. I just look down and see all the orange barrels. Here in our city, one road or another always seems to be under construction. For some time, a highway that leads to and from my neighborhood has been one of those filled with orange barrels and workers in hard hats.

Not long ago, a team of workers finished construction on the highway next to my neighborhood. And for some reason, the last stage of their job involved putting up "No entry" signs at the edge of that highway ramp right next to our subdivision. They changed the final fifty feet of the highway into a one-way street, so no one can legally enter or exit there. Instead, we have to take another road and travel the long way around.

You'll notice I said, "No one can *legally* enter or exit there." I must admit that most of us, including me, ignore the "No Entry" signs, take the shortcut, and enter and exit our neighborhood the same way we've done for years. Because of the recent changes, that means we now travel the wrong way on a one-way street.

Every time I commit this traffic offense, I feel guilty. But I can't say I feel shame. I don't stay up all night thinking about it, and my guilt doesn't hit me every time I get behind the wheel. Yes, I'm breaking the law, and most of the time, I'm sorry about it. But I'm not losing any sleep over my guilt, either. And I certainly can't say it has turned into the kind of shame that makes me unable to face someone else. Of course, I can't say I look forward to hearing the roar of a siren or seeing those flashing blue lights, either.

Guilt is a powerful force. But not as powerful as the shame that guilt becomes when we internalize it.

Work It Out

Through Jesus, God has made a way for us to deal with our guilt. But, lost in the downward spiral of the orphan heart, we think we can fix that guilt on our own. We can work out our guilt, we can work out our shame, and we can work out the problems of the past.

That's why so many people follow religions of works. If I can do something to pay for my sin, then I can take care of my guilt and shame without going back to my Father. Think about the pilgrimages to Mecca made by Muslims; the sweat ceremonies of some Native American religions; or the sacrifices to Agni, god of fire, in the Hindu religion.

Not long ago, I was leading a mission team in the city of Guadalajara, Mexico. There, I saw a poignant example of people attempting to work out their shame. A cathedral in the heart of this city houses an important statue of Mary known as Nuestra Señora de Zapopan (Our Lady of Zapopan), which many believe has been endowed with the spirit of Mary, the mother of Jesus. That day in October, what I noticed was not the statue, but the people who were following her because of shame and guilt.

Once a year, the petite (approximately one-foot-high) statue sets out on a journey. Attendants place her in the back window of a new car that has never been started, keeping it as a "virginal" car. Men then drag the vehicle by ropes from the cathedral in Guadalajara to the statue's home in the Basilica of Zapopan, eight kilometers away. More than 100,000 people turn out for the annual trek, celebrating with drums, flutes, and native dances planned for this special occasion. If you see the Virgin through the window of the car, they believe, you'll be blessed.

Miles away from the Basilica of Zapopan, lines are marked out on the cobblestone streets that lead to the church. These lines set forth the path for the penitent, who crawl behind the car to reach the Virgin once she's safely on the altar. In this case, it's not the bigger you are, the harder you fall but the bigger your sin (or the bigger you perceive your sin to be), the farther you crawl.

I've watched people with their entire forearms, elbows, and knees covered in blood as they crawl to the Virgin. They've internalized the guilt of their sin, and their shame is so great they believe they must work it out in this horrific way. If they can punish their bodies and show God how serious they are about the wrong they've done, they believe He may see them and take care of their guilt. A thick trail of blood follows the Virgin's vehicle as these faithful people make their way to her altar.

But the blessed truth is that forgiveness doesn't depend on how much you punish your body. It doesn't depend on how many treks to the altar you make or how many donations you give. The only thing that counts is that you receive the forgiveness Jesus earned for you by the punishment He received on the cross. But in the eyes of her followers, the way to the Virgin de Zapopan is the way to freedom from guilt and from shame.

Guilt vs. Shame

Growing up, my three brothers and I spent as much time in church as we did at home. Mom played the piano for the services and taught Sunday School, while Dad served as a deacon. No matter what happened at church, the Moores were right in the middle of it.

And most of the time, I was right in the middle of it, misbehaving. A boy who sits next to his younger brother in the church pew feels compelled to punch him, elbow him, or find some other way to get into trouble. But invariably, I would look up from my mischief and catch my mother's eye.

Mom had a way of staring out from the piano bench that struck terror into my heart. In one stark moment, my entire young life flashed before my eyes. I was guilty, and I knew it. I straightened up and did my best to behave like a model citizen for the rest of the service, hoping against hope that my new, reformed way of behaving would somehow lessen the punishment sure to descend later on.

I was experiencing true guilt. The Holy Spirit was using the watchful eye of my mother to call attention to my sin and convict me. When we have guilt, we can confess it. Because of what Christ did on the cross, we can repent of our wrong deeds and know His forgiveness. And unlike most parents, He won't remember our sins anymore. 2 Corinthians 7:10b tells us that "the sorrow that is according to the will of God produces a repentance without regret." What Paul describes here is the kind of guilt that draws us near to our heavenly Father.

We might call shame *bad guilt*. And as we've seen, the enemy wants us to have shame. Rather than having us experience Holy Spirit-fueled conviction and confession, he wants to trap us in our sins. And of course, he wants to keep us there, depressed, discouraged, and deprived of direction.

Guilt leads to repentance, forgiveness, and freedom. Shame leads to insecurity, self-condemnation, and a continuing cycle of sin. Guilt says, "I did the wrong thing, but God forgives me." Shame says, "I did the wrong thing, so I'm a bad person who doesn't deserve God's forgiveness."

When we sin, God intends that our guilt lead us to repentance. But shame, the tool of the enemy, leads us straight to condemnation. The more we think about our sin, the worse we become. "I'm no good." "I never get it right," we tell ourselves and those who know us. But Scripture says just the opposite: "God did not send His Son into the world to condemn the world, but that the world through Him might be saved" (John 3:17, NKJV) and "Therefore there is now no condemnation for those who are in Christ Jesus" (Rom. 8:1).

You've probably recognized that when we move from conviction to repentance, from guilt to confession, we're listening to the Voice Above. The Voice Above always moves us to freedom. When we listen to the Voice Below, however, we end up lost in shame and condemnation. Our sins become bigger than the God who died on the cross to save us from them. The enemy tricks us into believing our sin is so great that God cannot possibly forgive us.

Before we know it, we're in bondage, and our sin becomes a stronghold. When the Holy Spirit brings conviction into our lives, we can do one of two things. We can take it straight to the Father and repent, or we can internalize it, pulling out our masks and heading for foreign lands as hiders.

Facetime

The apostle Peter understood those options. He experienced the true guilt of conviction when he denied his Master not once but three times (Luke 22:54-62). Only a short while before, Peter made a statement his heart could not back up: "Lord, with you I am ready to go both to prison and to death!" (Luke 22:33). The Voice Below spoke to Peter, and he responded in a way that hurt both his Master and himself. The end of this chapter paints a moving picture of Peter's guilt: "The Lord turned and looked at Peter. And Peter remembered the word of the Lord, how He had told him, 'Before a rooster crows today, you will deny Me three times.' And he went out and wept bitterly" (Luke 22:61-62).

When I misbehaved in church and looked my mother eye-to-eye, I felt the guilt of conviction. And when Peter looked the Messiah eye-to-eye, he felt the same way. Conviction reveals our nakedness. When others see it, we can either run away and hide, or we can run straight to Him.

After his great denial, Peter disappeared from the scene. In his face-to-face moment with the Master he denied, he became a hider.

Of course, Peter couldn't hide from Jesus any more than Adam and Eve could hide from the Father in the garden. In Mark 16, we read of Christ's glorious resurrection. I always wondered why the angel at His tomb tells the two Marys, "But go, tell his disciples *and Peter,* 'He is going ahead of you to Galilee; there you will see Him, just as He told you'" (Mark 16:7). But after I learned about hiders, I understood: Peter no longer considered himself a disciple. He was unworthy. He had denied Jesus. *All I can do is hide*, he thought. And he did.

He hid, that is, until Christ reached out to him in love: "Go tell the disciples *and Peter*." Can you imagine how Peter felt when the women pounded at his door?

"Peter, Peter, come out!"

Silence.

"Peter, Peter, we've got something to tell you!"

(muffled) "I'm not home."

"We know better than that! C'mon! We went to the Master's tomb today, and you'll never guess what happened!"

Slowly, God's kindness expressed through the faithful women pulls Peter out of hiding. Slowly, the Father's kindness leads him to repentance. And when he meets the resurrected Christ in Nazareth, Peter the denier and hider experiences His transforming power.

The Peter we see in Acts preaches bold sermons and watches thousands come to salvation. He's taken his guilt to Christ, allowed Him to deal with it, and moved forward into the purpose God had planned for him all along. Peter the hider is now Peter the preacher, Peter the leader, Peter the rock. And neither his life nor anyone touched by his message remains the same.

If God can forgive the one who denied Him at the cross, He can forgive you. True conviction leads to a release to do the things of God and to carry out His divine purpose for our lives. Once Peter saw himself as a disciple, not a denier, he could move forward into his purpose. But first, Peter needed to be secure in his identity.

The Orphan Heart never releases us to do the things of God. The Orphan Heart never wants us to fulfill our purpose. It wants to keep us in a downward spiral: *No Father, no identity. No identity, no purpose.* The Orphan Heart will grow bigger and bigger, making us less able to do the things of God than we are today.

When we don't have a purpose, we end up with no direction. Let's take a look at the next lie the enemy feeds us so that we, like Peter, can pull out of the spiral and into the abundant life He came to bring.

The Battle: Does guilt have you trapped? Ask the Holy Spirit to reveal any known or unknown sources of your guilt and list them on a piece of paper. Read each one aloud as you ask and receive God's forgiveness. Now, take time to burn the list in a fireplace, run it through a paper shredder, or dispose of it in another permanent way.

6—Worried Sick:
You have no hope for the future.

No father, no identity.
No identity, no purpose.
No purpose, no direction.

"Much-Afraid, don't ever allow yourself to begin trying to picture what it will be like. Believe me, when you get to the place which you dread you will find that they are as different as possible from what you have imagined, just as was the case when you were actually ascending the precipice. I must warn you that I see your enemies lurking among the trees ahead, and if you ever let Craven Fear begin painting a picture on the screen of your imagination, you will walk with fear and trembling and agony, where no fear is."—Hannah Hurnard, *Hinds' Feet on High Places*[1]

Matt's Story, Part II

The same day that we met with the Ethiopian church leaders, the enemy was really beating the daylights out of me. I could tell that my fear and hatred toward the Ethiopian people were growing.

That night, I woke up at 3 a.m. and finally went back to sleep at 6:30 a.m. I woke up at 7 and prayed, asking God to give me His heart, eyes, and mind for the people. I didn't want to struggle through the trip because of hatred. The Lord began to burden my heart: If you allow the fear to overcome the faith, you'll be ineffective for the gospel. But if you allow your faith to overcome your fear, I will use you in a mighty way.

The next evening, I told Chad, "I need to be transparent with you. It's humiliating, but I feel like God is saying I must humble myself before you and before Him. I need to expose the darkness to light and allow the light to consume it." He didn't seem shocked, so I continued. "I've had a hatred for these people. I've been nervous, scared, and frightened. All of that has caused me to have a true distaste for these folks. But I want to get it out in the open now."

Chad and I began to pray together, seeking the Lord as brothers in Christ. We probably spent an hour taking this before the Lord, and He began to move mightily. The rest of the trip was great. The Lord freed me from all the fear, all the worry. I was able to preach and speak to the people, and I know He used me. But after walking boldly, it was amazing how fast I cowered down to the enemy again.

It happened on our trip back home. We had to fly back out through Doha, Qatar, and we arrived in daylight. As we were riding the buses in from the tarmac, I was looking out and seeing mosques—it was crazy. A thought arose, If I voiced my faith and said, "Jesus Christ is Lord," I would probably get arrested or at least pulled aside for questioning. I would miss the flight.

Once again, the enemy worked fast. We were on the bus, standing up with the little loops you hold onto. I was hanging onto a loop with my right arm and wearing a long-sleeved jacket. I have a cross tattoo on my right wrist, and since I was holding onto the loop, my sleeve pulled down to expose the tattoo. I looked to my left, and there was a woman with a frown on her face and disgust in her eyes, which were dead set on my cross. Without even thinking, I put my arm down and shook my sleeve to cover my tattoo.

In the terminal, God reminded me of Peter's story when he denied Christ. People always have opinions about that. But I don't think they realize what

Peter was going through. Out of my trying to save my own skin, I denied Christ. Instead of looking at the woman with love and saying, "What do you believe?" or "How are you doing today?" and allowing the Holy Spirit to work, in my flesh, I covered up the cross and just ignored the prompting in my heart.

But right there, God said to me, "Just as I forgave Peter, I forgive you. Now make sure you walk the way you're supposed to walk."

"Walker," the message from my friend from the Ivory Coast popped up on Facebook. "There's something I don't understand."

"What's that, Bamba?" Of course, I wanted to help. Bamba had served as driver, guard, and cultural advisor throughout our medical mission trip. At the end of the trip, he told me, "I don't want to be a Muslim anymore." After a short conversation over a chicken dinner, he confessed his faith in Christ in front of his Muslim friends. "I believe. I believe Jesus is the Son of God. I believe He died. I believe He rose from the grave. Jesus is Lord!"

Now, he was devouring Scripture as fast as he could, growing in the Lord, and helping lead a home Bible study. He had read something that didn't make sense to him, and he saw me as his mentor in ministry.

"I don't know why the Bible says, 'Do not fear,'" Bamba told me. "If we have Jesus in our hearts, would that not be redundant? We have nothing to worry about if we know Him!"

In his simple, unschooled faith, my friend understood his Father. He had already read some of the many verses that tell us not to fear or worry. Psalm 34:4 says God has "delivered me from all my fears." Psalm 56:3, addressed to God the Father, says, "When I am afraid, I will put my trust in you." In 1 Peter, we learn we can cast all our anxiety upon Him, for He cares for us (1 Pet. 5:6-7). If we know and trust our Father as Bamba does, we don't need to worry. And that's something even a new believer can understand.

Sister Act

When I think of someone with a worry problem, I can't help but recall the biblical story of Mary and Martha. These two sisters were some of Jesus' best friends; in fact, the Bible says He often spent time at their home in the village of Bethany.

Imagine it: You hear a sharp rap at the door and move to open it. There stands Jesus. What would you do?

This happened to Mary and Martha near the end of the tenth chapter of Luke. The Bible says Jesus "entered a village; and a woman named Martha welcomed Him into her home" (Luke 10:38b). Since Jesus is God, that meant God was in the house. The Creator of the universe, the one by whom all things were made, the one who had the answer to everything, came in to Martha's living room and sat on the couch.

How would you respond?

Luke shows us two different reactions to the same event. Scripture places Martha's alongside that of her sister, Mary. As soon as Jesus entered her home, Martha went into action mode: setting the table, stirring the soup, mixing up bread dough, and more. Whenever and wherever Jesus showed up, He almost always brought a crowd along. So Martha had more than Him to think about. Her table, her reputation as a hostess, and her position in the community were all at stake. No wonder she focused on the many tasks that lay before her.

The next part of the story seems all but unbelievable. I can picture our friend Martha waving a long, bony finger at her Master: "Lord, do you not care that my sister has left me to do all the serving alone? Then tell her to help me" (Luke 10:40b).

Jesus may have been in Martha's house, but she was in His face.

At that point, if I were Jesus, I'd have played the fire-from-heaven card, or at least said something divinely sarcastic. My imaginary speech might have gone something like this:

"Martha, do I care? Let's see now: I left the heavenlies to live on earth as a man. I gave up all My power as the Son of God. Soon, after an unfair trial, a group of Roman soldiers will rough Me up, beat Me, and hang Me on a cross. There I'll die a horrific death so you can have an everlasting relationship with Me. Yes, Sister Martha, I think I might care just a little bit."

Driven to Distraction

If I were Jesus, that's what I would have told Martha. I can't imagine her having the audacity to ask the question she did. But Scripture gives us a clue about the reason behind her behavior: *"She was distracted"* (Luke 10:40a).

Do you know how many people sit in church services every Sunday morning, distracted? God's in the house, but they're on their iPads or smartphones. They're making grocery lists, checking their email, or scrolling through the Facebook news feed.

The enemy can't stop God from showing up, so he does the next best thing and distracts our attention away from His presence. Martha's distraction led to an uncomfortable state of mind and heart. As Jesus put it, she was "worried and bothered about so many things" (Luke 10:41b). The Savior recognized her lack of freedom. But instead of responding in the ungracious way I suggested, He spoke to her with loving compassion.

The assortment of things that bothered Martha tied her to the past. *That Mary! She never helps when I need her!* or *The last time Jesus was here, we almost ran out of food.* Her worries, however, tied her to the future. *How can I feed all these people? Doesn't Mary know we won't be ready to eat if she doesn't get up and help? What'll people say if I don't offer them something soon?*

Because Martha allowed the enemy to distract her, she missed the blessing of having Jesus in her home. And while Martha stomped around the kitchen, Mary sat at His feet, choosing, as Jesus affirmed, "the good part, which shall not be taken away from her" (Luke 10:42b). Martha knew who Jesus was, but she lacked Mary's deep, intimate knowledge of Him.

It seems obvious, doesn't it? Martha didn't get her identity from her relationship with the Father. *No Father, no identity.* Instead, she worked hard to prove she was the hostess with the mostest, the one whose house sparkled and shone, the one whose pies all had meringues with the curlicues pointing the same way. And although these activities had value, they were not the "good part" affirmed by our Savior. *No identity, no purpose.* And while Mary sat at Jesus' feet, Martha ran around in circles, trying her best to get everything done. Her lack of identity and purpose took her further and further into the downward spiral of the Orphan Heart. There, she was unable to carry out God's specific plan for her life. *No purpose, no direction.*

If poor Martha had only followed her sister's example, she would have recognized the truth: God was in the house. And because of His presence and power, everything else would work out fine.

Cookie Monster

Our family went to the local Target store one evening when our youngest son, Caleb, was about five years old. At the time, Caleb loved to make a game out of hiding underneath the clothing racks and having us find him. We'd gotten used to hearing his little giggle while he waited and seeing his cheek-splitting grin as he burst out from behind the racks.

Not long after we got to the store, Caleb went missing. We didn't think too much about it at first. We figured he'd done a better job of hiding than usual. But as we looked behind rack after clothing rack, our concern grew.

All of a sudden, my wife remembered a recent news item: "Two weeks ago, a little boy was abducted from this same store," she whispered, trying not to upset our older boy, Jeremiah.

Shaken to the core, I divided up my family. We'd conquer the store and find our missing son. I was combing my assigned aisles when it hit me: this particular Target opened into a grocery store on one side. And Caleb was always hungry. *Could he have headed into the grocery to check out the snack aisle?*

I crossed the store's threshold and looked toward the front. Almost right away, I saw Caleb. His small frame contrasted with the adults in the checkout line ahead of him. And, true to form, he was holding a bag of cookies.

A more thoughtful husband would have picked up the boy and taken him straight to his frantic mother. But curiosity overruled my good intentions. *What in the world is he doing? And how is he going to pay for those cookies?*

I decided to hang back and watch. My son carefully laid the cookies on the moving belt and waited as the cashier scanned the package. "One dollar and eighty cents," she told him.

"I don't have the money on me, but my father knows where I am, and he'll be here to pay for it," piped the little voice, full of confidence.

That was more than I could take. I strode over to the line, handed the cashier two dollars, scooped up my son, and carried him back to our waiting family. I don't remember if we let him have any of the cookies or not. But that day, Caleb taught me something: he knew his father. He knew that when Dad left a store, he always left through the checkout line. Caleb had accidentally entered the wrong store, but because he knew his father, he knew I would show up to meet his needs.

Worry says, "I don't know where to go. I don't know if my Father will take care of my needs." Faith—the opposite of fear and worry—says, "My father knows where I am, and he'll be there to care for me."

Not to Worry

When worry comes, we focus on our failures, inadequacies, and problems. When we fail to focus on God, we have to work out our problems on our own. The enemy convinces us that the more we can work, the better we can fix the situation. So we end up like Martha, worried and bothered about many things.

But when we face a problem, God doesn't want us to work it out. Instead, He wants us to *faith* it. Our problems shouldn't make us work more, but faith more. Like little Caleb in the checkout line, the better we know our Father, the better we know where to find Him.

That's what faith does. That's what true worship does. When your worries tie you to the future with bonds of fear, you're an orphan with no purpose and no direction. But when you allow your worry to turn your heart toward Him and His adequacy, you can't help but worship.

The essence of worry is unbelief. Jesus showed us this in one of the Bible's most famous passages about worry, Matthew 6. Here, He says, "For this reason I say to you, do not be worried about your life, as to what you will eat or what you will drink; nor for your body, as to what you will put on. Is not life more than food, and the body more than clothing?" (Matt. 6:25).

In other words, Jesus commands us not to worry. In the rest of the passage, He redirects our focus. We should not be anxious because we know our Father takes care of the birds, the plants, and the trees. As

His children, are we not worth much more than these? If God can take care of these small, insignificant things, how much more will He take care of us, the people for whom He sent His only begotten Son?

Of course, worry comes from the Voice Below. And as Jesus points out in verse 27, it accomplishes nothing. It can't add even one hour to our lives. Just a few verses later, He identifies the root of worry: "But if God so clothes the grass of the field, which is *alive* today and tomorrow is thrown into the furnace, *will He* not much more *clothe* you? You of little faith!" (Matt. 6:30).

The basis of all worry is unbelief. Like Martha, we assume one of two things: our Father is too small to take care of our problems or He doesn't care enough to do so. Both are lies from the pit of hell. And if we continue believing them, the enemy will use them to drive us further into the dangerous mindset of the Orphan Heart.

At Awe Star Ministries, God often lets us watch Him work in miraculous ways. While I was writing this book, we needed to replace one of our fifteen-passenger vans. We didn't need a new van, but we did need a reliable one. We planned to use it for mission work, taking groups of students to Dallas for missionary training or to serve in Mexico and back again.

We didn't have much cash saved up, but we didn't want to go into debt, either. Some people urged us, "Just borrow the money!" but I didn't want to presume upon God. Instead of hurrying to the bank, we decided to wait, watch, and pray.

I also posted about the need on Facebook. Within hours, a woman at a church where I'd spoken a few weeks earlier contacted me. Another friend had told her about a van she wanted to sell, the exact size we needed. Although it had many miles on the odometer, a mechanic confirmed that it was in great shape. After we checked everything out, only one problem remained: the woman's husband.

"I only have a certain amount to spend," I told her. "If he won't take that, we'll have to look elsewhere. I'm sorry."

That day, when her husband came home from work, our friend told him about our ministry and the need for a reliable vehicle. With fear in her heart, she asked him how much he would take for the van.

The number he told her was not what she expected. In fact, it was much less: a perfect match for our van savings account. And, as it turned out, the family was coming to Tulsa that weekend. They would be happy to deliver the van right to our door. So our savings account stretched to include not only the van but its delivery, too.

If we'd worried about how to get the money for the van, our worry would have tied us to the future, thinking our transportation problems were bigger than God. But because He allowed us to focus on faith, we were able to see His provision.

Maybe Martha's worry problem wasn't a worry problem after all. Maybe it was a faith problem instead. And lack of true faith is a central component of the Orphan Heart.

The Right Track

I can't leave the topic of worry without explaining another way those with the Orphan Heart differ from those without it. Orphans focus on their rights. But those who have their identity secure in their Father focus on relationships.

To help us understand this principle, let's return to Mary and Martha. Martha felt she had the right to demand her sister's help. That's why she approached Jesus with such boldness. But because Martha chose to spend her time in the kitchen instead of sitting at His feet like Mary, she may have missed a miracle. What if Martha hadn't prepared the meal? Jesus might have turned the family's water into wine or, better yet, multiplied her loaves and fishes to feed 5,000.

When you're bothered about the past and worried about the future, you try to tell your Father how to fix it ("Tell her to help me"). It may have seemed as though Martha focused on serving others, but in truth, she focused on herself: *What will they think about me? How will I look? How come Mary won't get up and help?*

We see this same behavior in another "perfect" child, the elder brother of the prodigal son in Luke 15. Remember his anger when his father held a party for his newly-returned brother? He felt he had a right to be angry; a right to a bigger, better party; a right to the same inheritance his younger brother had squandered.

The father didn't see these things as anyone's rights. Instead, he saw them as the outflow of a living, loving relationship with him. If Martha had felt secure in that relationship, she would have trusted Jesus to take care of the situation in the right time and way. If the elder brother had felt secure in that relationship, he would have trusted his father's decisions, too.

When we don't trust our Father, we cling to our rights. And when we cling to our rights, we ignore the relationships that matter most. Jesus spelled out the most important ones in the same chapter where we find Mary and Martha's story: "You shall love the Lord your God with all your heart, and with all your soul, and with all your strength, and with all your mind; and your neighbor as yourself" (Luke 10:27).

When we cling to our rights, we hurt our relationships with other people and with God. And when we cling to our rights, we label ourselves as orphans. If we maintain this mentality, we're likely to take the next step and try to become someone we're not. And that can lead to more problems—and still more evidence of the Orphan Heart. Let's examine this final area so we can begin speaking the truth into the lies that continue its downward spiral.

The Battle: Think of a specific person or situation that causes you to worry. Now, write out a short plan for facing this problem with faith rather than fear. Review this personal prescription whenever worry threatens.

7—Fake ID:

You should become somebody you're not.

**No father, no identity.
No identity, no purpose.
No purpose, no direction.
No direction, no destiny.**

"What if I were a pilot? Not an actual pilot, of course. I had no heart for the grueling years of study, training, flight schooling, work and other mundane toils that fit a man for a jet liner's cockpit. But what if I had the uniform and the trappings of an airline pilot? Why, I thought, I could walk into any hotel, bank or business in the country and cash a check. Airline pilots are men to be admired and respected. Men to be trusted. Men of means. And you don't expect an airline pilot to be a local resident. Or a check swindler."—Frank Abagnale, *Catch Me If You Can*[1]

Dad's Story (as told by me)

My dad was sixty-five years old when we realized he didn't know who he was.

It happened when he went to apply for his retirement benefits. "This isn't your Social Security number," the clerk told him.

"But I've used it all my life. I used it in the Navy, when I worked—everywhere. I've always used that number!" Dad protested.

"We're sorry, Mr. Moore, but this number belongs to an Arvey Dean Moore."

"That's my brother!" Dad exclaimed.

"So why are you using your brother's Social Security number?"

"I've used it all my life! That's my number, not his!"

Before long, the story grew even more complicated. Dad finally had to track down his birth certificate. And when he did, it turned out he and his younger brother had the exact same name. For some reason, the doctor who delivered them several years apart had written the same name on their birth certificates, and no one had ever caught the error. At sixty-five years old, Dad had to go to court to get his name legally changed to the one he'd always used, "Orville Dean."

As it turned out, Dad's Social Security number was right, but his identity was wrong. For all those years—without knowing it—he carried around a fake I.D.

"I left home at sixteen, looking for me."[2]

Frank Abagnale, known as the world's most famous con man, wrote these words to describe his emotional state as he began a life of deceit. Between the ages of sixteen and twenty-one, he took on as many as one hundred different identities. And not one of them was real.

Abagnale successfully posed as an airplane pilot, a pediatrician, a college professor, and a tree surgeon. During this time, he also cashed $2.5 million in fraudulent checks in every state and twenty-six foreign countries. After the French police finally caught him, the master identity thief served time in the French, Swiss, and United States prison systems. "After five years, he was released on the condition that he would help the federal government, without remuneration, by teaching and assisting federal law enforcement agencies."[3]

In his memoir, *Catch Me If You Can* (later made into a movie starring Leonardo DiCaprio and Tom Hanks), Abagnale explains how he successfully defrauded airline employees, hospital staffs, and an unsuspecting public. For the past forty-plus years, he has served as an expert on check fraud, embezzlement, and identity theft, giving lectures to the FBI and serving private clients by instructing them how to reduce their risk of fraud, forgery, and embezzlement. He explains,

> The crime of this century is identity theft. It is so easy to assume someone else's identity. By assuming someone else's identity you can obtain a credit card in their name, get a car loan in their name, get a mortgage or a second lien in their name, or even go to work for someone as contract labor and have someone else be responsible for your taxes. We have given away so much information that anyone anywhere can become anybody at any given time.[4]

But, as we've seen earlier in this book, identity theft is just as big a problem in the spiritual realm. The enemy of our souls wants to steal our identity as honored children of a loving Father. He wants to kill our abundant life. And He wants to destroy the glorious destiny God has planned for our lives.

Sweet Spot

By this time, we recognize the downward spiral of the Orphan Heart. First, the enemy causes us to question our identity. Before long, we lose our purpose. From there, we end up without a direction. And in that damaged state, we have a hard time moving into the destiny God has for us.

Jesus succinctly expresses the contrast between the enemy's plans and God's desire for our lives: "The thief comes only to steal and kill and destroy; I came that they may have life, and have *it* abundantly" (John 10:10).

A key part of the abundant life is the God-given gift of *dominion*. Dominion happens when creation comes into sync with the Creator and walks out His purposes and desires. It's our sweet spot, the place where we experience the most joy, peace, and fulfillment. When we operate in our dominion, we experience a sense of freedom as we do nowhere else.

Several years ago, I was scheduled to speak at a church over the course of a weekend. When I arrived Friday afternoon, I asked the pastor about the conference schedule. "Give us everything you've got," he said. "Teach as long as you want. Just run with it."

It was a Bible teacher's dream come true. When I arrived home Sunday afternoon, I told my wife, "It was great! They gave me so much freedom. I could start whenever I wanted—even before breakfast. And they all seemed eager to learn. I taught a total of twenty-four times!"

"Awww," Cathy said, rubbing my shoulders with wifely sympathy. "You worked so hard this weekend!"

"No I didn't," I told her. "I didn't work hard at all! In fact, I had a twenty-fifth lesson ready, but I had a plane to catch."

In case it's not obvious by now, teaching is my dominion. It's my area of giftedness and joy, the place where life fits best for me. When I taught that weekend, I knew I was in the center of what God created me to do. I could work all day at teaching and it would never become a chore. It's not drudgery to me, it's absolute life.

When I teach, I move into the way God designed me and the gifts He gave me. And when I step outside of that, something's missing. Yes, teaching is my dominion.

Tug of War

Satan's goal, of course, is to make us orphans. He wants to draw us into his world so we won't experience the joys of life with the Father.

And pulling us away from our dominion is one way he tries to accomplish this.

God, on the other hand, wants to move us toward our dominion, that sweet spot where we become free indeed. We're in the middle of a tug of war, with Satan using his tricks to pull us away from our heavenly Father and toward his evil kingdom. He uses guilt, shame, worry, and anxiety to make us live as orphans.

Jeremiah 31:3 gives us the heart of the Father: "The Lord appeared to him from afar, saying, 'I have loved you with an everlasting love. Therefore I have drawn you with lovingkindness." The love of God pulls us toward our dominion and into our ultimate destiny of a loving life with Him. But how can He draw you in if you believe He's broken?

The reason so many of us fail to walk in the center of God's will and don't enjoy the fruit of the Holy Spirit is because we're walking around with Orphan Hearts. If we believe our Father is broken, we have no desire to respond to Him. The child of abuse is never drawn to the father's "Come here." He fears he will be hurt, abused, belittled, or demeaned.

The other day, I saw an angry woman in the grocery store. After she finished yelling at her little boy, she snapped, "Now, tell your mom you love her." Her son drew back in fear. And that's exactly how someone with an Orphan Heart perceives God. We know He's God the Father and yes, we're supposed to love Him. But we also believe He's waiting to smash us with a big stick.

Daddy 911

When my oldest son was three years old, he developed a sudden illness. Within only a few hours, he went from happy and playing to the sickest child I'd ever seen. Severe vomiting and diarrhea turned him into a concentration camp victim, his face drawn, his little ribs poking through his T-shirt.

What should we do? Cathy and I were terrified. We'd just moved to Dallas for a new ministry position. We didn't even have a doctor yet. Where could we take our too-sick little boy?

Through our church connections, we found a pediatrician who agreed to examine Jeremiah. When he did, his words were curt: "Get him to the hospital as soon as you can."

Of course, we rushed him to the Emergency Room, where blue-gowned medical personnel began performing all sorts of tests. Cathy and I kept reassuring Jeremiah, "They're going to make you better. It'll be all right."

But in a few minutes, they pulled him from our arms. "We're taking him for a spinal tap."

I watched my little boy disappear down the hall, his arms stretching back toward me. The farther away they took him, the more agitated he became. "Wait!" I called out. "This will go much better if I hold him."

"But a spinal tap—well, Mr. Moore, it's not an easy thing."

"I understand. But I want to be there for my son."

Once Jeremiah was back in my arms, he relaxed. Throughout the painful procedure, I held him close, and he did great. When you per-ceive your father as loving, caring, and protecting, you can get through any experience—even a spinal tap—just fine. But if you have an Or-phan Heart, you'll feel all alone on the sidewalk, and even a skinned knee will feel like a spinal tap.

Misattached

In the first chapter of this book, we talked about a psychological term called Reactive Attachment Disorder, or RAD. This syndrome occurs when biological orphans have an inability to form a true bond with the significant adults in their lives. I pointed out that the Orphan Heart is the spiritual equivalent of RAD. When we suffer from the Orphan Heart, we don't trust others enough to make firm attachments. Instead of trusting in our father the way little Jeremiah did, we pull away from him.

When we pull away, though, we tend to place that attachment somewhere else. Like the Prodigal Son running to foreign lands and embracing values apart from his family's, we reject the healthy attachment God wants us to have and turn to one or more of what author Jack Frost identifies as seven false attachments. You may notice some overlaps among them, and that's normal. But they're one of the best ways I've seen of breaking down the Orphan Heart into understandable chunks, so I'll use his terms and add my own explanations.

Position: For a long time, I moved toward this attachment. You may remember that although I loved my dad, I could never seem to please him. Our poor relationship helped drive me toward an Orphan Heart. Dad told me I would never amount to much. And of course, I set out to prove him wrong.

One day, while I was serving as the youth minister here in Tulsa at First Baptist Church, something exciting happened, so I called my dad to share the good news. "Dad! Guess what? Today, my peers elected me President of the Metro Youth Ministers' Association."

"What's that?" he growled.

"It's a think tank made up of youth ministers from the top fifty churches across the country. We're trying to make a difference in the youth ministry of America. It's such an honor, Dad. "

"Well, maybe. But you've never been a *real* pastor."

I shook my head as I hung up the phone. Dad didn't get it. And somehow, I knew he never would.

I was experiencing the same thing I've witnessed in the lives of CEOs from some of the largest corporations in America. They push and push, rise to the top of a company, have everything they've ever wanted, and it's not enough. Position alone cannot satisfy us because God did not create us for position. He created us for Himself.

People: The second false attachment the enemy uses to draw us is *people*. When we move toward people instead of our Father, we put them in His place. In other words, we try to derive our identity from them instead of from Him.

Orphaned men will try to conquer women so they can think of themselves as what we used to call the BMOC (Big Man on Campus), the strong, powerful, desirable one. And orphaned women will often give themselves to men they shouldn't. "My dad never connected with me emotionally," said one young mother. "And the love that you lack, you try to fill with whatever comes your way. There's nothing more humbling than having to tell your future spouse some of the stuff you've done."

Either way, having your affection and attention drawn to people instead of the Father is wrong. And it's another sure evidence of the presence of the Orphan Heart.

Places: This third false attachment is one we've already mentioned several times. Like the Prodigal Son, we often attach ourselves to far-away places instead of to our Father. I meet pastors who go to place after place, church after church, in an attempt to find their identity. They need the big church on the big block in order to be happy—or so they think. But the housewife humorist, Erma Bombeck, had it right in the title of her book: *The Grass Is Always Greener Over the Septic Tank.*

A new church won't satisfy. A new city won't satisfy. And as long as we're substituting a place for a closer relationship with our heavenly Father, we'll remain on the move.

Performance: When it comes to attachment, perfect children (the modern-day equivalent of the Prodigal Son's elder brother) take this route. Since they can't please their father (or another significant adult in their life), they think they can reach their sweet spot of dominion by pleasing other people instead. This type of person becomes a pleaser, doomed to please not just one person but everyone in the room. And of course, their task is impossible. Sooner or later, one of the plates will stop spinning or one of the balls will tumble down. And for the pleaser, just one displeased person or one dropped plate equals failure. If pleasers can't have it all, they want nothing. That's the ultimate dominion of the Orphan Heart.

Possessions: When we attach ourselves to a possession, we've got to have it, no matter what *it* might be. We start accumulating all sorts of toys, thinking the more we have, the bigger we'll win. But all we end up with is a mountain of toys and no win in sight.

In my years of working with high school and college students, I've seen this attachment often. Students are always looking for one more possession to make them cool or hip. The iPhone 4S isn't good enough anymore; it has to be the iPhone5. They can't live in the world with last year's model, or they don't feel good about themselves.

Some people use their possessions in an effort to move them toward a particular position. That's the overlap I mentioned at the beginning of this section. But the main place an attachment to possession moves us is deeper into the Orphan Heart.

Power: Have you ever met someone who, no matter what the situation or circumstance, always has to one-up you? This person is almost always a victim of the Orphan Heart, and almost always attached to power as a means of finding fulfillment.

Right after I returned from carrying the cross up Mount Kilimanjaro, I met a man for the first time while we sat together in a place of business. I had to apologize to him for nodding off during our brief conversation. "I just came back from Africa, and I'm still getting over the jet-lag," I told him.

"I've traveled all over the world, too. What were you doing in Africa?" he asked.

"This year, I had my fortieth anniversary in the ministry. I took a team of men, and we celebrated by carrying a cross to the top of the highest free-standing mountain in the world."

"Is that right?" he said. "Yeah, I've done all that stuff—mountain-climbing, the whole bit." And off he went on a story of his own exploits.

This man reminded me of the little boys who play King of the Hill. They keep pushing one another down until there's only one left on top. Orphans like this have to be bigger, stronger, and better than everyone around them. They can't allow someone else to win for fear they won't look as strong.

Please don't get me wrong. Every little boy is born with the desire for power. And we do need leaders. Someone has to be the alpha male or King of the Hill. The problem comes when we attach ourselves to power as the source of our identity. And yes, the problem comes from the Orphan Heart.

Passion: Almost any type of addiction falls into this category of false attachment. Scripture says that "God...richly supplies us with all things to enjoy" (1 Tim. 6:17). But when the enemy moves us to make that enjoyment an obsession, we start looking for our identity in the things we love. Alcoholics find their identity in a bottle. Sex addicts find theirs in all sorts of deviant behavior. And where do you think we got the term "comfort food"? Yes, that macaroni and cheese or chocolate chip cookie makes us feel good. But only for a little while.

Attaching ourselves to a passion is like scratching an itch: the more you do it, the more you want to do it. And you can never take care of the itch because it's caused by something below the surface. All the scratching you do up on top won't touch the problem below. And before long, your enjoyment has become an obsession, and your passion, an addiction.

The more time addicts spend with the object of their passion, the deeper their addiction grows. But addictions never satisfy us in the deepest part of our lives because our destinies do not lie in their fulfillment. God designed us instead to find both our identity and our true fulfillment in only one place: our fellowship with Him.

Identity Confusion

"We love your son!" the childcare worker at Glorieta, a national conference center, told my wife and me as we picked up Caleb that afternoon. We were attending a training session for youth pastors, and both Caleb and Jeremiah had activities to keep them busy during ours.

"Yeah, Peto's a great kid!" another worker chimed in. "He keeps everybody smiling!"

"Bye, Peto!" another boy told him.

"See you tomorrow, Peto!" said someone else.

Cathy and I just looked at each other. *Peto?* We knew a Peto, but he wasn't a member of our family. Peto was Caleb's best friend back home. So you can imagine the questions we had for our son once we left the childcare area.

"Aww, I just like that name," he told us. "I think it's cool, so I told everyone my name was Peto."

Without any criminal intent, our son had taken on Peto's identity as his own. And although he didn't have a fake ID to back up his claims, people continued calling him "Peto" for the rest of the week.

But true identity confusion is more than a childish game. Sometimes, our identity becomes so mixed up that we don't know who we are, where we belong, or what we do. Since we have no direction, we can't step into the destiny God planned for us.

And who creates such confusion? None other than the enemy himself. Do you remember the temptation of Jesus? Matthew records that it took place right after He spent forty days fasting and praying in the desert, a time of total intimacy with God.

The first two times Satan threw out a temptation, he prefaced it with the words "If you are the Son of God." The first thing the tempter did was to try to attack Jesus at the place of His identity. The Greek word for *if* used here means "Since." The enemy had no confusion about Jesus' identity. But he was trying to instill doubt within Jesus—the same thing he tried to do with Adam and Eve in the garden, and the same thing he tries to do with us today.

Jesus had no questions and no confusion about His identity. In fact, He's the supreme example of the opposite of the Orphan Heart, for which I use the biblical term *sonship*. But don't worry: you don't have to be male to have sonship. All you have to do is rest in your Father's love.

Jesus knew His Father loved Him. He was secure in His identity as the Son of God. That's why, even though Satan tempted Jesus with power and possessions—two of the seven false attachments—He stood firm.

If Satan's #1 attack on Jesus was at the point of identity, how do you think he attacks us? Most of the time, we get our identity not from whom God has created us to be, but from whom the world thinks we are. The next step happens when we start believing that lie. If all a child hears from his parents is, "You're stupid. You're dumb. You're no good," it doesn't take long for him to see himself as stupid, dumb, and no good. That's when, in regard to our identity, the Voice Below becomes the Voice Within.

Once you understand your true identity, you have the freedom to move into your dominion. Identity defines who you are, but dominion determines what you do. If identity is the rock dropped into a pond, dominion represents the rings spreading out from that rock. What God created you to do has a direct correlation to your identity in Him. And all those rings lead to the ultimate destiny and fulfillment of every believer: an abundant life in Him.

But why do so many believers fail to experience that life? You already know the answer: because of the Orphan Heart. In the next chapter, we'll explore one final lie Satan uses to keep us from God's abundance.

The Battle: Which of the seven false attachments (position, people, places, performance, possessions, power, and passion) has most tempted you? Ask God to help you renounce this attachment and cling only to Him.

8—Death Sentence:

Life's not worth living.

No father, no identity.
No identity, no purpose.
No purpose, no direction.
No direction, no destiny.
No destiny, no life.

"I can't deceive myself that out of the bare stark realization that no matter how enthusiastic you are, no matter how sure that character is fate, nothing is real, past or future, when you are alone in your room with the clock ticking loudly into the false cheerful brilliance of the electric light. And if you have no past or future which, after all, is all that the present is made of, why then you may as well dispose of the empty shell of present and commit suicide."—Sylvia Plath, *The Unabridged Journals of Sylvia Plath*[1]

Allison's Story (as told by her mother)

I'll never forget that warm spring evening. And of course, I'll never forget my little girl.

I could hardly wait for nighttime to come. My husband and I had dinner plans with one of his clients, but that didn't seem like anything special.

But the opportunity to have my whole family together again made this weekend extra-special. My two sons were coming in from college, and their little sis-

ters looked forward to their visit as much as Mark and I did. Allie and Amanda stayed home for the evening, putting the last-minute touches on the house while waiting for their brothers to arrive. Hoping for an early end to our dinner, I kissed them both goodbye as we headed out for the restaurant.

During the meal, I missed a call from a friend. When several text messages followed, I excused myself from the meal and called to check things out.

What I learned horrified me. Allison, our sixteen-year-old, had skipped school that day and, unbeknownst to either family, spent it at the beach with their son. We'd known his family for years, but he and Allison weren't boyfriend and girlfriend. As far as I knew, Allie wasn't interested in anyone. She knew Mark and I encouraged group activities and wanted our children to save dating relationships for later. Two years ago, she'd made a firm commitment to purity. With pride, she wore the silver ring her father gave her at the church ceremony where the students made their commitments public.

The friend who called me sounded angry, and I understood why. Our children had betrayed both our trust and theirs. Allison and I needed to talk—and fast.

Before I stepped back into the restaurant, I made a quick call. I wouldn't ream her out over the phone. I knew better than that. But I was upset enough about this that I felt I had to let my daughter know her little secret was no longer a secret at all.

"Young lady, we need to talk," I told her. "And you may as well turn off your phone and leave it on the kitchen table. You won't be seeing it again for a while."

Allison didn't say much in response. Looking back, I would say that her silence said it all. I breathed a quick prayer before I rejoined my husband and his clients. We ate as quickly as possible and made our excuses. I didn't tell Mark the reason for my abrupt departure from the table until after we'd said goodbye.

On the way home, we got another phone call. Only this one would change our lives forever.

"Mom! It's Allison!" Jonathan choked out. "I found her out in the barn. She . . ." he broke down.

Our other son, Jeremiah, picked up the phone. "Mom, I called 911. They're on the way. Mom, it looks bad. Really bad."

By the time we drove the remaining few blocks to our house, the flashing lights of the ambulance lit up the Missouri night. I ran to my child, already strapped to a gurney. "Allie! Allie! You know Mommy and Daddy love you! Baby, what were you thinking?"

Allie was still alive, but she couldn't respond. Mark pulled me away from her and, his hands shaking, helped me into the ambulance to make the ride with my baby. I didn't cry, but I did pray. Perhaps God knew I needed to save both my strength and my tears for the days to come.

Our sweet baby girl lived for just six more hours, long enough for all of us to tell her good-bye, long enough for me to ask forgiveness for my harsh tone, long enough for me to start wondering "Why?" and "What if?" I didn't know how my words would move her to take such a drastic step. I didn't know where she had found the gun. And I didn't know why she had done what she did.

All I knew was that, in a moment of foolish thinking, my daughter listened to the wrong voice. In skipping school and spending the day with the young man, she made a foolish mistake. But in taking her life, she made a permanent decision. And none of us will ever be the same.

If there was ever someone in the Scriptures who should have had no doubt about his destiny, it was Samson. In Judges 13, we read about his birth.

As the story opens, his mother is barren; she "had borne no *children*" (Judges 13:2). But the angel of the Lord appears and tells her she will have a child. Not just any child, of course. Her son will be a "Nazirite to God from the womb" (Judges 13:5), an enduring identity.

A Nazirite was someone "appointed" or "set aside" to the Lord. Nazirites did not cut their hair, eat or drink grapes in any form, or have contact with dead bodies. One could take a Nazirite vow for a particular season or purpose, much as we set aside a time of fasting and prayer today. Or, like Samson, one could be appointed as a Nazirite for life.

Oh, Baby

Folded into Samson's setting-apart was a purpose designed just for him. Right after the announcement that the not-yet-expected baby will be a Nazirite came the words, "and he shall begin to deliver Israel from the hands of the Philistines" (Judges 13:5c). Note that the Scripture didn't say He *would* deliver his people, only that he would "begin to deliver" them. We'll come back to this later. But God was setting apart this special baby to play a unique role in his people's battle with the Philistines, their oppressors for the past forty years (Judges 13:1). That had to be good news.

What does all this mean? Before he was born—before he was even conceived—Samson was set apart. He had a father: Manoah. He had an identity: he was set apart as a Nazirite. The way he walked, talked, dressed, even the way he ate and drank matched that special vow. He had a purpose: to deliver Israel from the Philistines. He had a direction, the specific path in which God would lead him to carry out His will.

When we live out our identity, our purpose, and our direction, they always lead us to our destiny, which will always bring glory to God. But destiny is like a coin: it has two sides. One side is our individual destiny, tied in with our personal calling, abilities, and spiritual gifts. The personal side of my destiny coin will look different than yours, but if we flip them both over, we see the glory of God.

Wise Manoah recognized the responsibility of raising a child with this unique claim on his life. He didn't hear the original announcement, so he asked God to send His messenger again "that he may teach us what to do for the boy who is to be born" (Judges 13:8b). God responded to the request by once again sending the angel to Samson's mother.

After the future mother realized her surprise visitor returned, she went to get her husband so he could meet the answer to his prayer. Next, Manoah and his wife received their very own *What to Expect When You're Expecting* instructions straight from the hand of their heavenly Father.

Moving On

It seems clear that from the moment of his conception, Samson had a special anointing and appointing. God's plan was perfect. But in Judges 14, some of Samson's character flaws emerge. Although his identity and purpose were clear, he didn't choose to follow God's specific direction for his life. Like the Prodigal Son, he chose to go to foreign lands and seek his own way.

Timnah *was* a foreign land for Samson, and not just because it was a different country. It was also the land of the hated Philistines. It also ended up being the site of rejection, the place where Samson walked away from both God and his parents. Like many of us, he found himself in the wrong place doing the wrong thing with the wrong people.

Once he arrived in Timnah, Samson fell for the first pretty girl he saw. His parents unsuccessfully tried to remind him of his calling and that a girl from the enemy tribe was probably not his best choice. But Samson, like a spoiled child, demanded that his parents "Get her for me, for she looks good to me" (Judges 14:3b). Clearly, Samson went to the wrong place.

From this point on, Samson chose to live not according to his principles or purposes but according to his passions. His lack of direction meant his life could not—and did not—line up with the destiny God intended for his life.

Samson shouldn't have married anyone for her looks alone but someone who shared his belief in the one true God. And now, we watch Samson progress through the downward spiral of the Orphan Heart. He returned to Timnah where, the Bible says, he was "in the vineyards" (Judges 14:5b) when a lion attacked him. In an amazing demonstration of strength, Samson ripped the wild beast apart with his bare hands. But the Bible also reports that he "did not tell his father or mother what he had done" (Judges 14:6).

Why did he keep this secret from his parents? Because his Nazirite vow said he would abstain from grapes or grape products. He shouldn't have visited the vineyard, and he knew it. Samson was in the wrong city, the land of the Philistines, and in the wrong place within the city, a vineyard. And in this wrong place, at precisely the wrong time, a lion sprang to attack him.

The enemy, who "prowls around like a roaring lion" (1 Pet. 5:8), wants to take us away from our Father and move us to the wrong place to do the wrong thing. He loves to lead us to the place of secret sin—the most devastating place we can go.

Sweet as Honey

Next, we catch another glimpse of Samson's downward spiral. While on his way to be married, he saw a swarm of bees in the carcass of the lion he had killed earlier. Just like Martha, who could have been sitting at Jesus' feet but thought she had too much housework, Samson became distracted. As a Nazirite, he couldn't touch anything dead. So what did he do? He decided to disobey his vows, scoop out some of the sweet honey, and take it home to his parents.

Doesn't all sin look sweet in the beginning? Samson gave the honey to his parents but again failed to tell them about the lion. Once again, he chose the direction of secret sin. And once again, he exhibited numerous qualities of the Orphan Heart.

Next, he did something else Scripture advises against: mocking at sin (Prov. 14:9). He turned the honey-in-the-lion story into a riddle, thinking he could use it to win himself some new clothes (Judges 14:13-14). The identity, purpose, direction, and destiny God laid out for him was so different than what we see him doing here. Samson failed to embrace his identity and his purpose. And when we do that, we go to wrong places and start doing wrong things.

When Samson's questioners, the Philistine men, couldn't answer his riddle in three days, they came to his wife for the answer (Judges 14:15). In his attempts to make us fall, the enemy loves to use the people closest to us. Samson's wife became manipulative, combining her words with tears in an attempt to get him to reveal the correct response (Judges 14:17).

Samson could kill a lion with his bare hands, but he couldn't stand up against his wife's tears. He could conquer others, but he couldn't conquer himself. The enemy had captivated him, and that captivation led him further into destruction.

Samson lost the bet with his new Philistine friends, which meant he had to give them thirty changes of clothing. Instead of going to the Timnah Fashion Outlet, however; he went down to the battlefield and killed thirty men. This quick method of debt reduction led to one more violation of his Nazirite vow. Here, he was not touching one dead body, but thirty.

Catching Fire

Samson had progressed from secret sin to blatant wrongdoing. His attachment to his passions was becoming an addiction, and he was exhibiting more and more characteristics of the Orphan Heart. How many times have people gotten hooked on alcohol, gambling, or drugs and then stolen from friends or family to cover their losses? Like others whose affections overpower them, Samson was trapped in a desperate, downward spiral.

In Chapter 15, Samson learned the terrible truth: Because of his negligence, his father-in-law gave his daughter, Samson's wife, to another man. And now, Samson took out his rage in an inappropriate way. Men with Orphan Hearts don't just get angry; they get even. And for orphans, "even" isn't good enough. They have to be one up, one more, one better than everyone else. For Samson, this meant tying 300 foxes together by the tail and then setting fire to the tails so the Philistines' crops would burn. God had called him to destroy the Philistines, but not in this way or at this time. He was walking outside of God's direction and thus failing to move into his destiny.

Next, the Philistines showed up at the camp of Judah, ready to avenge themselves against Samson. Our hero's own people, anxious to separate themselves from his radical behavior, bound him with two new ropes and turned him in to their enemies. Enraged, he again displayed supernatural strength, and the bonds dropped away. He then took the jawbone of a donkey and used it to kill 1000 more Philistines. How ironic that, after walking away from the identity, purpose, and direction God gave him, Samson now attempted to walk in obedience by taking matters into his own torch-bearing, jaw-wielding hands.

In the midst of his disobedience, Samson became thirsty, asking God to bring him something to drink. Does his behavior remind you of ours? We drive over the speed limit, then pray for God's protection. We head to a party with heavy drinking, then ask God to keep us from harm. Samson was in the wrong place at the wrong time with the wrong people, but when he needed help, he called on the name of the Lord.

God blessed this right choice, and Samson moved into a twenty-year period where, the Bible says, he "judged" Israel (Judges 15:20). As is often the case, the Hebrew word carries special meaning. We think of a judge as someone who makes decisions, who weighs the evidence and issues a verdict. But *judge* as used here means *deliver.* So in this season of his life, despite his mistakes, Samson walked in the purpose and direction God had for him.

We don't see the details of that twenty-year period, but once it ends, we again find Samson in a foolish attempt to display his strength. He removed a gate and transported it to the top of a mountain in Hebron, a distance of some forty miles. Did God intend him to use his strength in such a foolish pursuit? Of course not.

One-Trick Pony

Like Samson, we often take God's good gifts and use them to perform useless activities. We waste what He has given us and follow directions with no meaning or kingdom value.

This reminds me of a story my wife likes to tell. Cathy grew up outside the city limits of Hannibal, Missouri—the home of Mark Twain. Her dad ran one of those old feed stores you see in movies of rural America. Like every other little girl, she longed to have a horse. She knew her family had plenty of land behind their house, and the horse could eat the grass that grew there. But in their area, just owning a horse was a luxury. And luxuries were something only rich folks could have.

One day, a man from the city approached her dad about renting some land. He had just bought a horse and needed a place to keep it. Cathy's dad saw a chance to do two good things: earn some money and provide a way for his little girl to fulfill her dreams.

The man agreed, and the horse was delivered. You can imagine the excitement of a young, horse-loving girl waking up to discover that one has been dropped into her backyard. Cathy had visions of riding across the pasture at full gallop, her little body bouncing in the saddle and her long, blonde hair flowing behind.

But sometimes our dreams don't match reality. Instead of a horse, the animal Cathy's dad had agreed to keep turned out to be a tiny Shetland pony. He was so short that when Cathy's brothers tried to ride him, their legs dragged the ground. And this pony also had an unusual habit: he only walked in circles.

You see, this animal had spent most of his life traveling with kiddy circuses—the kind that set up in a grocery store parking lot, erect a tent, and harness five or six ponies to a treadmill-looking contraption. Parents pay a small fee so their children can sit on a pony as it walks in a circle.

The only thing this pony had ever known was little children straddling its back as it walked around and around. And whenever Cathy tried to ride, the pony would walk in the same tiny circle. No matter what she did, it seldom broke its pattern. There was no long gallop across the field, no beautiful hair flowing behind—just plodding along in a circle, day after day, ride after ride.

The enemy's goal is to turn our lives into parking lot pony rides, and we settle for his tricks. Instead of walking in freedom and power, we waste our time plodding around in circles or moving gates. And like both the pony and Samson, we end up far away from our Father, far outside our identity, far away from God's purposes, far off in the wrong direction, and far removed from using our destiny to bring glory to God.

The Biggest Loser

But Samson went even farther from God's plan than the circling pony as he moved into a codependent relationship with the gorgeous Delilah. The enemy knows our weaknesses better than we do. And in the same way he used Samson's first wife against him, he now used Delilah. Like her predecessor, she attempted to get him to give her information for the Philistines to use against him.

Once again, Samson was moved not by his identity, not by his purpose, not by his direction, but by his passions. He lied to Delilah about how he could lose his strength, but he was the one who was truly deceived. At this point, Samson has traveled far off the right paths God laid out for him and moved further toward his ultimate destruction.

The further we get from what God has designed us for (our identity, purpose, and direction), the more we come in bondage to cheap substitutes. We see this as after Delilah discovered Samson's secret: his strength lay in his uncut hair. After she sheared it, she cried, "The Philistines are upon you!" (Judges 16:20a). And all too soon, Samson found himself both blind and bound. He had already lost the life-vision God laid out for him. And now, he lost his physical vision as well.

Samson lost his vision: He became blind. He lost his vitality: He became weak. And he lost his victory: He became enslaved. Not long afterward, he made the decision to snuff out the lives of his enemies by bringing down the pillars, ending his own life in the process. No direction had led to no life. Samson had lost it all.

In his life, Samson made bad choice after bad choice. But he remained confident of God's protection. In Judges 16:20c, we see one of the saddest sentences in Scripture: "But he did not know that the Lord had departed from him." God's presence was no longer with him, and he failed to recognize it.

If we keep living an orphan lifestyle, holding onto our Orphan Heart, there will be a day when we end up just like Samson. When the Voice Below becomes the Voice Within, we develop a stronghold. We walk away from the light and embrace the dark. We step outside of our dominion and move into self-destruction. Although Samson had godly parents, the enemy stole his identity, killed his purpose in life, and destroyed his direction. Samson fell into the downward spiral of the Orphan Heart, and instead of the destiny God intended him to have, the enemy took him to its terrible, logical conclusion: no life.

Living Dead

But you don't have to commit suicide to have no life. Sometimes, a living death can be worse than a physical one.

I know someone trapped in a living death. Her name is Michelle. She attended high school in our area many years ago and was one of the most beautiful, godly young women there. To this day, if you ask Michelle what she wants to do with her life, "Be a missionary," is her immediate response.

Michelle had just entered high school when her policeman father was killed in a drug bust. And after the loss of her father, everything changed. To find fulfillment, she began to look for relationships with other men. When she was only fifteen, she ran off with a boyfriend. Before she knew it, she was on the streets as a homeless, pregnant teenager, and the boyfriend was nowhere in sight.

Michelle has what I call the Samson Syndrome. God gave her an identity and purpose in life, but she stepped away from it and has never been the same. Still a teenager when her baby girl was born, she raised the child to adulthood with many missteps along the way.

Today, you can find Michelle in one of three situations: strung out on drugs and alcohol, in rehab, or in a church working to earn God's favor. The intimacy she missed out on when her father died she now tries to find in other men. She moves from one place and relationship to another, trying to find something that will satisfy her. If you asked her how many men she's slept with, the answer would number in the thousands.

Michelle sensed God calling her as a missionary as a young girl. And of course, her father's loss was a tragic event. But Michelle has never waited for God's provision to meet her needs. Instead, like Samson, she keeps taking shortcuts. Her life has become a living death. And until she gains freedom from the Orphan Heart, she not only has no identity, no purpose, and no direction, but even without committing suicide, she has no life.

Orphaned—or Not

Can you see it now? Michelle couldn't, and Samson couldn't, because the lies of the enemy had blinded them. But when your Father speaks your identity into you and you know your purpose, your direction and destiny become clear. When you have the opportunity to make decisions at key points in your life, your continuing fellowship with your Father guides you into the right choices. And right choices will lead to the direction and destiny that match His desires.

But when you reject your identity, as Samson did, you reject God's purpose for your life. When it comes to making decisions, if you aren't considering His desires ("Does this decision take me toward my destiny or pull me away from it? Is it lined up with God's direction or with the enemy's? Is it toward life or away from it?"), you can't go in His direction and move toward the destiny He has planned.

When you remove the destiny component from your life, you do whatever seems right at the moment. You make decisions in the flesh, temporal choices rather than eternal ones (Judges 21:25; Prov. 21:2).

When Samson rejected his identity and played around with God's purpose for his life, he made decisions contrary to the direction that would allow Him to fulfill that identity and purpose. Remember? He went to the wrong place at the wrong time with the wrong people. He went to the vineyard and missed the victory. He made a joke out of his identity as a Nazirite and a mockery of the specific purpose and direction God gave even before he was born.

It's so easy for us to look at Samson's life and ask, "Why?" Why would he turn against his parents and his heavenly Father? Why would he disobey his vows? Why would he make any one of what must have been hundreds of choices that turned him away from God and toward destruction, away from life and into death? Samson, of all people, had an identity, a purpose, a direction, and a destiny.

But so do we. More often than not, we identify ourselves as orphans when we're not. That's why I call the Orphan Heart the biggest lie. Despite the fact that he had a loving father, the Prodigal Son perceived himself as an orphan. And, since he thought he had no father, his decision-making process was based on a lie. He didn't consider his true purpose, direction, or destiny. And neither did Samson. And neither do we.

The enemy feeds us the lie: *"You don't have a father who loves you."* But the reality is that, just like Samson, we do. And we have an identity, purpose, direction, and destiny. We don't have to end up like Michelle, living the zombie life as the walking dead. We don't have to end up like Samson, dead in the rubble of our lives. We can move out of the Orphan Heart and into the health and wholeness of the abundant life.

It all begins with a choice to move toward the Father. Let's learn together how that can happen.

The Battle: Samson's life and death show the sad downward spiral of the Orphan Heart. How could he have used the tools of spiritual warfare to counteract the lies of the enemy? Today, when the enemy tempts you to hear his lies, ask God to help you use your own weapons to protect yourself from harm.

Section III.
The Truth that Sets You Free

9—Redeemed:
You matter because you matter to God.

"When at last she was free to come back to Edmund, she found him standing on his feet and not only healed of his wounds but looking better than she had seen him look—oh, for ages; in fact ever since his first term at that horrid school which was where he had begun to go wrong. He had become his real old self again and could look you in the face. And there on the field of battle Aslan made him a knight."—C. S. Lewis, *The Lion, The Witch, and the Wardrobe*[1]

Emily Bo's Story

My story begins when I was a sophomore in high school. Like every other girl, I struggled with self-image, self-worth, and just not seeing much value in myself.

One of the biggest issues was that I didn't feel love very easily. And of course, the enemy would tell me lies: "Your family members only love you because they have to. No one really loves you because you're worth anything." That was a big issue for me. And those things progressed and intensified. I had thoughts like, "You're not beautiful," "You're not smart," or "You're not pretty."

It just progressed to where I couldn't look in a mirror. There was nothing about me physically or even emotionally that I cared for. It got to a point in my sophomore year that I contemplated suicide or self-harm. I would lock myself in the bathroom, cry out to God, and wish it could be different. I didn't actually believe what I knew to be God's Word.

I went to Panama on an Awe Star mission trip the summer between my sophomore and junior year, and that was my breaking point. No one knew about any of this—not my parents, not my friends, no one. It was just something God and I were struggling with. During that week in Panama, the night after Walker gave the Orphan Heart message, I just broke. I was talking with God and saying, "I can't do it. Something has to change. Either my thoughts about myself have to change and I've got to get better, or I'm going to break." I couldn't really be strong anymore.

I talked with some of the girls in my room first, telling them what I was going through and having them pray for me. Then, the next night, I talked to Walker. I really poured my heart out about everything I was struggling with. He looked me in the eye and said, "You're not Emily to me anymore. I'm not going to call you Emily. Your new name is Bo. Do you know what that means? It means 'beautiful one,' and that's not just what you are, it's who you are. To me, to all the people on this team, and most importantly, to God—that's who you are."

We cried, and he reassured me. It's been a process after that, but God is so good and so faithful. That new identity is so reaffirming; it's just been incredible.

It was a struggle, because after having that experience, I couldn't go home and not talk about it. None of my family knew about anything that was happening in me for the past year, so I had to talk with my parents and tell them everything. That was difficult, but definitely a good part of the healing process. And just letting people in was a big thing—letting people see the broken so it could heal.

You know how Walker has you look in a mirror? I still do that, and say, "I am the beautiful one." Something happens when you hear it out loud and you speak it about yourself. It's still a struggle—I think every person struggles with it—but the process is a beautiful thing.

When you're secure in your identity, your perspective on life changes—just like Emily Bo's. But how do we move into that sort of confidence?

Once we know Jesus as Savior, Satan can't take away our Father, because we are sealed and secured in Him. But the enemy doesn't want anyone to live as a part of God's family. He wants to make us orphans in the Father's house. Remember Jesus' promise in John 14:18? "I will not leave you as orphans; I will come to you"? Let's review the reason He made it.

Triple Play

God loves you. God loves you. In fact, He loves you so much that He wants you to be a part of His family. And He loves you so much that He provides three different ways for you to enter in.

On October 7, 1951, I was *born* into the O.D. and Katie Moore family in Marshall, Missouri. From that day forward, I've been a part of the Moore family. Because of that, I have uncles, aunts, nieces, and nephews. I have a father who provided for me and a mother who took care of me. That's one way you can enter a family: by birth.

But you can also be *adopted* into a family. That's such a wonderful way to begin your family life. Adoptive parents long for a child. They desire parenthood so much that they're willing to do whatever it takes to bring a child into their home. And once that child has a home, he or she experiences the same benefits as the other family members.

The third way of becoming part of a family is to *marry* into it. Little did I know that when I married Cathy Silver on December 20, 1974, I wasn't just marrying my beautiful wife. All of a sudden, her family became mine. Almost right away, I had to buy Christmas presents for my new parents and siblings. I had to attend all kinds of Silver family events. The Moore family is Irish, but the Silvers' ancestors came from Norway. Before long, Cathy and I visited some of her family in Wisconsin, rich in Norwegian heritage.

I felt like I'd stumbled into a Muppet movie. "Velcome, Valker, to Visconsin," her family members told me over and over. Yes, it's vonderful—I mean *wonderful*—to belong to a family.

But the enemy doesn't want us to have that warm family feeling. In fact, he doesn't want us to feel as though we have a family at all. He wants to make us feel like outsiders, with no rights to the blessings and benefits of family membership. He wants to steal our joy in attending family events.

He wants us to feel like orphans. He wants to give us Orphan Hearts. And He wants us to forget our Savior's promise: "I will not leave you as orphans. I will come to you" (John 14:18).

Who's Your Daddy?

As I shared earlier, our Awe Star teams work in orphanages across the globe. Often, I visit the facility ahead of time to do some set-up work for an upcoming visit. But do you know what's funny? The same thing happens almost every time. As I stand there talking to the director or other orphanage official, one or more orphans come running up to me and grab my leg. "Daddy, Daddy," they cry. They use their own language, but I know the words. And I know the pain.

These children want someone they can call father. When an orphan says in his heart, "I have no father," he knows if he did have a father, he wouldn't leave him in that institution. A real father would rescue him. So an orphan tells himself, "Because I'm in this place, I have no father. And since I have no father, I have no home. I'm surrounded by other children who also have no father. And we're all waiting for the day someone—anyone—will come and tell us, "I'll be your father, and I'll give you a home with me."

Having a home is a good thing. When I was a college student, I couldn't wait for breaks, because then, I got to go home. I got to sleep in my own bed, eat my favorite foods, and enjoy time with my family. But an orphan has no home, no place, and nowhere to go.

Even after we become children of God, the enemy wants us to feel and act as orphans. So those with the Orphan Heart walk around living as though they have no Father, no identity, and no home. They've bought into the biggest lie.

What God wants us to know is that He loves us so much that He's taken care of it all, three times over. Everyone who enters His family comes by birth. And that's exactly what He told Nicodemus, Jesus said, "Truly, truly, I say to you, unless one is born again he cannot see the kingdom of God" (John 3:3).

But everyone who enters the family of God also comes by marriage. In the book of Revelation, Jesus is described as the groom, and we (the church) are his bride. That's just another term to describe us as children of God. God so loved His children that He's coming back to get all of us and bring us to be with him forever. "Let us rejoice and be glad and give the glory to Him, for the marriage of the Lamb has come and His bride has made herself ready" (Rev. 19:7). In fact, the Bible describes this time as a "wedding feast" (Matt. 22:3). We always need a place to go home. And in the picture of the marriage of Christ and His church, God has provided just that.

Finally, everyone who enters His family comes by adoption: "Just as He chose us in Him before the foundation of the world, that we would be holy and blameless before Him. In love He predestined us to adoption as sons through Jesus Christ to Himself, according to the kind intention of His will" (Eph. 1:4-5).

When parents adopt a child, they have to go through a complicated process. Social workers come and study their home. They examine the environment, the financial background, and more. The prospective parents endure a great deal to find out if they're deemed worthy to receive a child, and then, their names go on a waiting list. Some people wait for years, and some never get a child at all. But in every case, the parents, not the child, initiate the adoption process.

Adoption begins much the same way in the spiritual world. The Father is the one who seeks the child, not the other way around. And God, as the prospective parent, has done the same thing: He has paid a great price—the blood of His only begotten Son—to adopt us as His children.

God had such a deep desire for you to be part of His family that He provided all three ways—birth, marriage, and adoption—for you to become one of His children. That's how much He loves us. God the Father loves each of us so much that He sent His Son Jesus to die on our behalf. It's the Father who wants to bring us back into the fold. And it's the enemy who doesn't want us to have a deep, lasting knowledge of how much our Father loves us.

For years, when I thought about the Father's love, I thought about my earthly dad. And although I knew my father loved me, I also thought I had to work for his love. This gave me a false picture of my heavenly Father. And Satan used this false picture to give me an Orphan Heart.

God's intention in creation was that every father would demonstrate His love in such a way that we wouldn't have to make a big leap to go from earth to heaven, from our human father to our heavenly Father's love. But because we live in a broken world, our image of the

Father has been tainted. Because fathers don't know how to live out this image, most of us have difficulty understanding the Father's love. He loves us deeply. He loves us greatly.

If the enemy can keep you from the Father's love and all the abundant life He has for you, you'll spend your life as an orphan. That means you'll have no identity, no purpose, no direction, no destiny, and worst of all, no life.

But of course, the Bible offers hope, truth, and a way back to the Father. Let's look at two different orphans who found their way to Him.

A Tale of Two Orphans

In John 3, we meet a man called Nicodemus. Nic had all the things the world could give him. His good friend, Joseph of Arimathea, provided Jesus' tomb. Only wealthy people owned tombs, but Joseph had one. And no doubt, Nicodemus' wealth rivaled that of his friend.

But despite his material worth, Nicodemus had a need. He had possessions: he was wealthy. He had position: he was a leader of the community. In fact, he probably had all of the seven P's (seven false attachments) people with an Orphan Heart tend to pursue (See Chapter Seven). But he also knew something was missing.

We may recognize something is missing in our lives, too. But we don't often know where to go for the answer. We don't know who to talk to. And we may not know what questions to ask. But Nic knew. God gave him insight and intelligence enough that he took his need and his questions to Jesus.

Instead of coming to see Jesus during the day, as most people would, Nic made his visit under cover of darkness (John 3:2). No doubt, he wanted to avoid the stigma of a high-ranking Pharisee coming to see the Master. But Jesus didn't criticize or condemn him for dropping in after hours. He also gave Nic the simplest of answers: "You must be born again" (John 3:7b).

With these few words, Jesus was saying, "You're an orphan. You have all the possessions, the position, the power, but you're living without a father and without a home. Nic, the Father wants you."

But another favorite biblical story, found in Luke 19, makes a great contrast with Nic's: the story of Zacchaeus, the "wee little man" of the children's song. As a wealthy, influential Pharisee, Nicodemus was living the high life. Zacchaeus, as a tax-gatherer, was known as a lowlife. Nic was the perfect child, and Zac was the prodigal.

Just as no one today gets excited about a visit from an IRS agent, no one wanted to see Zac. Everyone knew tax collectors charged more than the law required so they could skim a percentage off the top. No one friended them on Facebook or followed them on Twitter. In short, almost everyone thought highly of Nic, but no one thought of Zac. No one at all.

As short in stature as in reputation, Zac had heard about the man passing through town. He'd never met Jesus, but it seemed everyone else was talking about Him. And now, Jesus was visiting Zac's hometown of Jericho.

The word on the street penetrated his office. When he stepped outside to check on the situation, he couldn't believe what he saw. The crowd spilled across the main road and onto the side streets, across the side streets and onto the surrounding hillsides. How could a little man like Zac hope to catch a glimpse of this stranger who, some people said, claimed to be the Son of God?

Zac looked at the huge sycamore beside the highway and, in an instant, he knew: The tree would give him the height God hadn't. He could rise above his peers and satisfy his curiosity all at the same time.

Unlike Nic, Zac didn't intend to have an appointment with the Savior. But when Jesus reached out and commanded him to "Come down" (Luke 19:5), he made the right choice. And when Jesus visited his home, Zac again made the right choice. He told Jesus, "Behold, Lord, half of my possessions I will give to the poor, and if I have defrauded anyone of anything, I will give back four times as much" (Luke 19:8b).

Jesus spoke the truth: Salvation had come to this house and to Zac, just as it had to Nic. Both now had a Father. Both now had a home. And both could now walk in sonship instead of living under the shadow of the Orphan Heart.

If you haven't become part of the family of God, you have the opportunity to do that right now. You see, we're all Nics or Zacs. Like Nic, we may have a nice house and a wonderful family, but deep down, we know there's something missing. We've done all the right things, but we don't have all the right answers.

Or maybe we're like Zac. We've taken the easy way out, but it's proven harder than we thought. Making wrong choices has failed to lead us to right ways of living. And the fun we found in breaking the rules doesn't seem like so much fun anymore. Like Zac, we may feel we've been set aside, alone in the fig tree while everyone else dances in the streets.

In the same chapter as Nic's story, John 3, God tells us He loved the world so much that He sent His only Son, Jesus, to save us from the wrong things we've all done. And as we've discussed, whoever receives this gift becomes part of the family of God by birth, marriage, and adoption all at once.

Are you a Nic or a Zac? Either way, if you've never made the decision to follow Christ, you need to be born again. Would you pray with me, please?

Dear Jesus, I confess to You that I'm a sinner. I've done many things that deserve punishment. Please come into my life, save me, and be my Lord. I give my life over to you. I want my way to become Your way, and I will follow You all the days of my life. In Your holy name I pray, AMEN.

Princess Power

We all long to feel important, to know we matter to someone. For the past few years, I've spent nearly every summer in Panama, working both in the cities and in the tribal villages. One day, I was standing near one of our ministry sites in Panama City talking to one of our interpreters, Isaac. He was telling me about the lives of the many street children we see. I was still dressed in the king costume I wear to participate in *Freedom*, the pantomime drama presentation we use to share the gospel.

While the interpreter and I were talking, I felt a sharp tug on my pants leg. A little girl stood there, yanking at my clothing and speaking in rapid Spanish. I motioned Isaac over to translate our conversation.

As it turned out, my young friend had only one question for me: "Can you really make me a princess?"

"Yes, I can."

I pulled out my PVC pipe sword to tap her on the shoulder as I pronounced her a *princesa*, but she flinched. I knew the look in her eyes—the look of the wounded. She hadn't received kind treatment, so she didn't expect it. Where I meant to give a blessing, she anticipated a blow. So holding my sword close to my side, I knelt down to continue our conversation.

"Let me tell you about a Father who will never hurt you." And so I shared with this precious child about the Father who really loved her, the Father who had wonderful plans for her life. And she listened. Boy, did she listen.

As my little friend grinned from ear to ear, I stood back up and gently laid the sword down to touch her shoulder. "I now pronounce you a princess, the princess of Panama City and of God's Kingdom," I told her. And as quickly as she had come, she ran off, laughing.

About thirty minutes later, we were doing ministry about half a mile from the place where I met the new little princess. All of a sudden, I felt a familiar tug on my pants leg. My new little *princesa* was back. And this time, she brought her five-year-old brother along.

"He wants to be a prince," she said with confidence.

So we went through the whole procedure again. That day, I anointed both a prince and a princess. And I pray that one day, they'll come to know the King of kings.

Worth It

But how does God measure our worth and value? I began to understand this as the result of my favorite religious TV program, *The Antiques Roadshow.*

One day, I tuned in the program, and a farmer came clumping into the spotlight, wearing overalls and carrying a small writing desk. He set it down in front of the appraiser.

"Where'd you get this desk, sir?"

"Bought it at a garage sale."

"How much did you pay for it?"

"Five dollars."

"Why did you buy it?"

"I have a twenty-seven-inch TV, and I was looking for a twenty-seven-inch desk to put it on. This fits."

The appraiser began looking at the piece. Before long, he was examining it from all sides, turning it upside down and pulling out the small drawer in the front. Finally, he asked the owner, "Sir, do you know we've been looking for this desk for a long, long time? We knew it existed, but we didn't know where it was."

The farmer grunted.

"This desk has rarity. It's one-of-a-kind. It's unique."

Another grunt.

The appraiser continued, "And I know whose desk this is."

"Mine," the farmer said. "I paid five dollars for it."

"No, the man who made this desk put his name on it." He turned the table over and pointed to a spot near the back, revealing the name of Paul Revere carved into the wood.

"Paul Revere made the desk himself, and it came from his home. Do you know how much it would go for at auction?"

"Five dollars. I paid five dollars for it."

"No. The auction would start at a quarter-million dollars, minimum bid. And we don't know where it would end. So what are you going to do with the desk now?"

"Take it back home and put my TV back on it."

As I listened, I began to understand how God sees us. First, we have rarity. We are "fearfully and wonderfully made" (Ps. 139:14). He created us unique, with no two of us alike.

Second, we have the Maker's name stamped on us. We're created in His image. Just as my shirt collar bears the name of the maker, every individual has a stamp, "Handmade by God."

I was at a church in Missouri teaching this lesson when I picked up a guitar from an onstage stand. "How much is this guitar worth?" I asked the musicians.

"$1200," a guitar player told me.

I picked up a second guitar, identical to the first. "And how much is this one worth?"

"$1200. It's the same kind of guitar."

"But wait a minute," I said, as I peered down into the guitar. "I see a name written here. It says, umm, Elvis Presley. Yes, Elvis Presley's name is written on the inside of this guitar. How much is it worth now?"

"All the money I have," said the guitar player.

Just like the guitar, the One whose name we bear changes our value. What once seemed common and ordinary is now precious and priceless.

But *Antiques Roadshow* also taught me one more way to measure worth and value: how much someone is willing to pay. How can we estimate the cost of one drop of Jesus' blood? He is the One who died to take away the sins of the world. In order to buy us back, He paid the ultimate price. Our worth is immeasurable.

Who Matters to God?

But in spite of how much God says we're worth, the Orphan Heart often prevents us from understanding or embracing our worth and value. Like the little Panamanian prince and princess, we all need affirmation. We all need to know we matter to someone.

The enemy, via the Voice Below, wants to tell us that everybody *else* matters to God. But not us. We've sinned too much. We come from the wrong background. We aren't smart enough, gifted enough, or special enough.

With the enemy's cooperation, we can all come up with many reasons God shouldn't care about us. And of course each of these is contrary to Scripture. We've already gone over the truth that He loves us so much He sent His only Son to die for us. As Revelation 1:5 reminds us, He is the one "who loves us and released us from our sins by His blood."

But because so many people think they don't matter to God, I decided some time ago to do a study about who does matter to Him. After examining only a few passages, I was amazed. All sorts of people matter to God.

I decided to put some of my findings into a list. Next to each person or group of people are the Scriptures that relate to that specific entry and a brief summary to remind you of the person or story.

I encourage you to take your time to read through this list and look up the accompanying verses. Like me, you may be surprised at all the people who matter to the One who matters most.

People Who Matter to God	Scripture	Summary
Blind	Mark 8:22-25	Blind man at Bethsaida
Children	Mark 9:36-37	Little child among disciples
Condemned to Death	Luke 23:32-43	Thief on the cross
Crying/Grieving	Mark 5:38-49	Talitha's family and friends
Dead	Mark 5:41-42	Talitha, dead little girl
Deaf	Mark 7:32-35	Man who couldn't hear or speak
Deformed	Mark 3:1-4	Man with the shriveled hand
Demon-Possessed	Mark 1:21-28	Man in synagogue at Capernaum
Desperate	Matt. 8:5-13	Centurion with ill servant
Divorced	John 4:7-26	Woman at the well
Educated	Luke 2:46-47	Teachers in the temple

Fearful drowning	Mark 4:35-41	Disciples, afraid of
Feverish	Mark 1:29-31	Peter's mother-in-law
Hemorrhaging	Mark 5:25-34	Woman who bled for twelve years
Hungry	Mark 6:37-44	Feeding of the 5,000
Imprisoned	Heb. 13:3	Those in prison
Lepers	Mark 1:40-42	Man with leprosy
Married	John 2:1-11	Wedding at Cana; water into wine
Mixed-Race	Luke 10:25-37	Good Samaritan
Paralyzed	Mark 2:1-12	Lame man with four friends
Parents	Mark 9:17-25	Father with demon-possessed son
Poor	Matt. 25:31-46	Hungry, thirsty, sick, strangers, etc.
Rich	John 3:1-21	Nicodemus
Royal	Acts 26	Paul before Agrippa and Bernice
Sick	Mark 6:5	People healed in Nazareth
Short	Luke 19:1-10	Zacchaeus
Unclean	Luke 17:11-19	Ten lepers
Widows and Orphans	James 1:27	Definition of pure religion

I haven't included the final verse and category on this list. John 3:16 makes it clear that everybody matters to God. But the Voice Below wants to make us think everybody *else* matters to God. Orphans, widows, poor people, rich people—all sorts of people matter to God, and we can embrace that idea. But we have a hard time transitioning from a list like the one we just examined to understanding deep inside that we matter to God. The Orphan Heart puts up a huge barrier that keeps us from full acceptance of God's love.

Examine the list again. If God can love all these people, why wouldn't we think His love includes each of us? We must make a leap of faith from believing God loves everybody to knowing God loves me. How can a holy God who created the universe, who hung the stars in place and created the sun and moon, find time to love an individual? This is where we must ask our heavenly Father to help us accept by faith what the Bible says is true: *We matter to God.*

If you find yourself still having trouble with this concept, I'd like you to speak the truth (and against the biggest lie) with me right now. Yes, it's all right. In fact, I think it will mean more if you speak the words out loud: *I matter to God.*

You may hear all sorts of voices whispering to you: *No, you don't. You're damaged goods. You've sinned. You've done wrong.* But if He could love the least of these, you're not as far away from God as you think. And as we've seen, what we think and feel is often very different from what God says.

Those who don't follow Christ are all walking around with Orphan Hearts. Of course they don't have a Father, an identity, a purpose, a direction, or a destiny, because they don't have Him at the center of their lives. But the sad truth is that so many of us who claim Christ's name also carry the Orphan Heart.

The devil has done his handiwork well. He's convinced many of us to buy into his lies and to live as if we don't matter to God. Let's keep working together to escape the lie: to turn away from the Orphan Heart and back to Him.

The Battle: God's Word is a strong weapon of warfare. Ask a friend or family members to hold you accountable to memorize Psalm 139:14-18 to help you combat the lie that says you don't matter to God.

10—Reclaimed:

You are your Father's favorite child.

"Soon the Ragman saw a woman sitting on her back porch. She was sobbing into a handkerchief, sighing, and shedding a thousand tears. Her knees and elbows made a sad X. Her shoulders shook. Her heart was breaking.

The Ragman stopped his cart. Quietly he walked to the woman, stepping round tin cans, dead toys, and Pampers.

"Give me your rag," he said so gently, "and I'll give you another."

He slipped the handkerchief from her eyes. She looked up, and he laid across her palm a linen cloth so clean and new that it shined. She blinked from the gift to the giver.

Then, as he began to pull his cart again, the Ragman did a strange thing: he put her stained handkerchief to his own face; and then *he* began to weep, to sob as grievously as she had done, his shoulders shaking. Yet she was left without a tear."—Walter Wangerin, "Ragman"[1]

Holly's Story (a letter to Walker Moore)

[Holly, a pastor's daughter, chose the path of rebellion as the expression of her Orphan Heart. For some time after college, she worked as a campus representative for a beer company, promoting alcohol use among college students. When she lost that job, she moved back home with her parents, uncertain of what to do

with her life. During this time, Walker Moore heard her story and invited her to travel with a group he was leading on a mission trip to Mexico.]

Dear Walker,

It's been a little over a week since I've been home and I am still trying to process everything that happened on my trip to Mexico. What an amazingly awesome trip! And although I was very glad to get back home (I slept for the first three days back) I believe that my time spent in Mexico was one of the best experiences I've ever had.

I really can't express how honored I feel that you invited me to assist you. I was so blessed by your leadership and your guidance throughout the trip. I don't know how to put my gratitude into words. I want to thank you for talking and listening to me about the all the stuff that I've been through. I hold your words in the highest regard. I felt like my eyes were truly opened when you spoke of the Orphan Heart. I had felt so lost (like I had no purpose or direction) because I had shunned my Heavenly Father. I now know that everything that I have been through in the past year was God's way of slowly preparing me to finally "get it."

I also got so much from the time you spoke at the church in the village about God taking away your guilt from the past and your worry about the future. One other thing that really hit me on this trip was what I have been taking for granted. There were so many people who heard the message we brought who were so thankful. Many of whom probably never had heard about God's love before. But me, I had the gift of hearing about God's salvation from the day I was born. I was raised with the privilege of knowing Jesus, and yet I still turned my back on Him. What a selfish life I have led, to take my relationship with Jesus Christ for granted when there are so many people who have never even heard of Him.

Walker, I don't know if I told you or not but one of the main reasons I said yes to this trip was because of you. Although I didn't really know you, I knew you were a godly man, and if you were offering me such an opportunity, there had to be a reason for me to go. I went into this trip scared, nervous, and unsure

*of even why I was supposed to be there. Today I can say that it was one of the best
experiences of my life! I know why God had me on that trip and I thank Him
every day for your faithfulness in praying for me to go for so long.*

> *With much love and respect,*
>
> *Holly*

We've discussed what the Orphan Heart looks like and how it affects people. But I believe we should also talk about what someone with true sonship looks like. The only One who never succumbed to the Orphan Heart is Jesus. Let's look at His life as an example and see how His sonship affected the way He grew up.

Did Jesus know His Father?

That's an important question. And according to Scripture, there's no doubt He did. God first pronounced sonship on Jesus at His baptism. "And behold, a voice out of the heavens said, 'This is my beloved Son, in whom I am well-pleased'" (Matt. 3:17). In addition, the first recorded words of Jesus in the New Testament were about His Father. In the second chapter of Luke, Mary and Joseph spent three days looking for their Son when He disappeared after a trip to Bethlehem. When they finally found Him sitting in the temple with the priests and teachers of the law, Mary rebuked Him as only a good Jewish mother can do: "Son, why have you treated us this way? Behold, Your father and I have been anxiously looking for You" (Luke 2:48b).

Although still a young boy, Jesus knew His Father and His identity, which gave Him both purpose and direction. His response says it all: "Why is it that you were looking for Me? Did you not know that I had to be in My Father's house?" (Luke 2:49b)

At only twelve years of age, Jesus knew His Father's house. In fact, He had already been invited into His Father's business. Jesus was secure in His relationship with His Father. That's why He could speak with such confidence to His earthly parents. Since Jesus never sinned, we know He was not being disrespectful. He was simply stating the truth and walking in His identity as the child of the King.

Now let's move to the end of Jesus' life. There on the cross, in His final moments of agony, we again find Jesus talking about His Father: "Father, into Your hands I commit My spirit" (Luke 23:46b). And how much did He talk about His Father between age twelve and His death on the cross? Throughout the gospel accounts, references to His Father fill the recorded words of Jesus. Let's take a closer look.

Jesus was secure in His identity.

In Matthew 4, when the Spirit led Jesus into the wilderness to be tempted, Satan launched a frontal assault. And the first thing He hit on was identity: "And the tempter came and said to Him, 'If you are the Son of God, command that these stones become bread'" (Matt. 4:3).

"*If* you are?" Satan may as well have said, "Do you really know who your dad is?" Just as he did in the garden with Adam and Eve, the enemy tried to bring about identity confusion. But Jesus knew His Father and trusted His Word. That's why He quoted Scripture back to Satan, saying, "It is written, 'Man shall not live on bread alone, but on every word that proceeds out of the mouth of God'" (Matt. 4:4b).

Because Jesus knew His Father, He remained secure in His identity. Later, when the Jews in Jerusalem challenged Him about who He was, He had a clear answer: "I and the Father are one" (John 10:30).

In Luke 10:22, when He spoke with a large group of followers, Jesus again made the connection with His Father plain. "All things have been handed over to Me by My Father, and no one knows who the Son is except the Father, and who the Father is except the Son, and anyone to whom the Son wills to reveal *Him*." Jesus knew His Father, and He spoke about His identity with anyone who would listen (and some who wouldn't).

Jesus knew His purpose.

In Scripture, no one had a clearer purpose than Jesus. John 10:10 reveals purposes for both the enemy and Jesus, "The thief comes only to steal and kill and destroy; I came that they may have life, and have *it* abundantly." He came to give us life, and not just life but fullness of life—abundant, overflowing life. Jesus knew His purpose. And because this was true, Jesus was never confused about the path He should take.

Years ago, when Awe Star Ministries was brand-new, a student named Daniel went with us to Hungary and Romania. One morning, he didn't feel good. "Daniel, I'm going to pull you out of ministry today," I told him.

"Walker, please don't. Let me go."

"Daniel, I just need you to rest. I want to take good care of you."

"Please, please let me go. I promise you won't be sorry. Please."

We had a busy day of ministry scheduled, and Daniel played the part of Jesus in our drama. You guessed it. I let him come.

During the drama, as Jesus hung on the cross, he threw up all over himself. The watching crowd was amazed. *Was that part of the drama?* Afterward, many of them wanted to find out.

"Why didn't you stop if you were so sick? Why did you keep going?" they wanted to know.

"I came a long way to tell you about Jesus," Daniel explained. "If I didn't keep going, you would never have heard about Him."

Daniel had a purpose that kept him going no matter what. A purpose helps us push through and rise above our pain. A purpose keeps us focused. A purpose moves us toward our direction and destiny. And a purpose helps us bring glory to God.

Jesus knew His direction.

After the Transfiguration, when those closest to Him seemed to grasp His identity, Jesus began to reveal His direction. "From that time Jesus began to show His disciples that He must go to Jerusalem, and suffer many things from the elders and chief priests and scribes, and be killed, and be raised up on the third day" (Matt. 16:21). Since Jesus knew His purpose, He also knew the specific path that would allow Him to fulfill it. When you know your Father, you know your identity. And when you know your identity, you know your purpose, so your specific direction is set.

Those of my generation all came of age in the '60s, and we set out to find ourselves. We rejected our fathers, so we struggled with our identity. We gazed at flowers, did LSD, and took all sorts of other trips in an effort to find it. We tried to teach the world to sing, but we couldn't get no satisfaction. We ended up in nowhere land listening to the sounds of silence.

When you have no identity and no purpose, you have no direction. But direction came to Jesus because He had those things in place. Jesus knew where He came from, so He also knew where He was going— even when others, like the scribes and Pharisees, didn't understand: "Jesus answered and said to them, 'Even if I testify about Myself, My testimony is true, for I know where I came from and where I am going; but you do not know where I come from or where I am going'" (John 8:14). Until we have a relationship with Him and the fellowship with Him that brings abundant life, we won't have direction. Once again, Jesus shows us the way because He is the way.

God loves us so much that He wants us to call Him by the Aramaic term for *Daddy*, "Abba" (Rom. 8:15). He wants to have the close type of fellowship with us that makes calling Him "Daddy" seems normal and natural.

Jesus knew His destiny.

When you have a father, identity, purpose, and direction, you have a destiny. I reached back into my Bible college days to pull out a couple of words that help me understand both Jesus' destiny and my own. Destiny is both *linear* (a continuing process) and *punctiliar* (a one-time event). We are walking out our destiny in order to reach the point of our destiny.

In other words, Jesus' direction was a part of His destiny. When He reached His destiny, He had done everything His Father asked Him to do, and because He reached it, even in death, He had life. When we walk in sync with the way the Creator designed us, and we find our identity in our heavenly Father, we find our direction and destiny. We are walking in life.

Unlike Jesus, none of us knows our final destiny, but we do know it involves walking out the life He has for us. We know He's leading us toward a particular point, and we know that point will bring glory to God. In Christ Jesus, we see a life lived out in all the right ways, one that follows a single purpose and goes in a direction to match.

But the enemy wants to break this chain and mess up things along the way. If he can snap it at the beginning, as soon as we have a relationship with God the Father, he will. He will steal, kill, and destroy to keep us from our ultimate destiny: an abundant life of walking with the Father. His goal is to make us think we have no Father. He wants to give us an Orphan Heart.

The Father's Love

Of course, the opposite of someone with sonship is someone who has an Orphan Heart. Even orphans, once they're old enough to understand, know they have biological fathers. But because they lack earthly contact, *father* is only an idea, not a reality in their lives.

The enemy wants us to live in that mindset of uncertainty. The Bible tells us that everyone knows God exists (Rom. 1:18-20). But the enemy doesn't ever want us to meet God, to have a relationship with Him, or to know how much He loves us. Instead, in an effort to confuse and mislead us even more, he tries to get us to redefine *love*.

If we have the wrong definition of love, we'll never understand the love that comes from the Father. My Baby Boomer friends and I all thought love was "Feelings" (whoa, whoa, whoa). But true love is not based on an emotion or feeling. Instead, it's based on a principle and a Person. The principle: "I choose to bring out the best God has for you without expecting anything in return." We see this principle at work in Romans 5:8, where God the Father acts as our example: "But God demonstrates His own love for us, in that while we were yet sinners, Christ died for us." Even while we were God-haters, God loved us enough to send His Son.

The Person on whom this principle is based, of course, is Jesus Christ: "For God so loved the world, that He gave His only begotten Son, that whoever believes in Him shall not perish, but have eternal life" (John 3:16). Most people don't deny the existence of God. And, whether or not they know Him, many would claim to be His children.

But in John 1:12-13, God says He has given His children every right to call Him the Aramaic term for *daddy*, "Abba." He wants to have such fellowship with us that calling Him "Daddy" seems normal, natural, and right. He longs for our hearts to cry out to Him as they do to our earthly fathers.

And this heavenly Father is the best father of all. He wants to have the kind of fellowship with each of us that helps move us forward into that *Abba* relationship. He wants us to crawl up into His lap and enjoy His presence. We can only do that when we are free from shame, guilt, and worry. And that can't be true for someone with an Orphan Heart.

Knowing the Abba side of God is to know the deepest truths about Him, to know Him as the true Father He is. This Father does not have the flaws and failings of an earthly Father. This Father doesn't change His attitude or behavior based on the circumstances, your actions, or how He may feel about you at the time. We need to know, as Paul said, "what is the breadth and length and height and depth, and to know the love of Christ which surpasses knowledge, that you may be filled up to all the fullness of God" (Eph. 3:18b-19).

Why was Jesus so attracted to His Father? Because He knew the true Father. And He wants you and your Heavenly Father to have the closest relationship any two people can have. When you can have that kind of relationship, it changes all the other relationships in your life for the better.

Because I lived for so long as an orphan, there were many things I didn't know about my heavenly Father. As we continue on our journey to freedom from the Orphan Heart, I want to share some of them in the following "Did You Know" Chart.

Did You Know?

Did you know there is nothing in heaven or earth
that matches our Father's love toward you?

Read 1 John 3:1

You have a Father who loves you.

Did you know the Father cares for you so much He
wants to walk alongside you and carry your burdens?

Read 1 Peter 5:7

You have a Father who cares for you.

Did you know you're the apple of your Father's eye?

Read Psalm 17:8

You have a Father who thinks you're His favorite child.

Did you know you're more valuable to
your Father than anything on this earth?

Read Matthew 6:26

You have a Father who thinks the best of you.

Did you know your Father has given you the keys to His place?

Read Luke 12:32

You have a Father who is generous.

Did you know your Father only gives you good gifts?

Read Matthew 7:9-11

You have a Father who lavishes His best on you.

Did you know your Father wants you
to call Him by His most intimate name?
Read Romans 8:15-16
Your Father wants you to call Him by His special name, Abba.

Did you know your Father knows
what you need before you ask Him?
Read Matthew 6:8
You have a Father who is proactive on your behalf.

Did you know your Father will do more
for you than you could ever imagine?
Read Ephesians 3:20-21
You have a Father who is extravagant in His love.

Did you know your Father is always thinking good of you?
Read Jeremiah 29:11
You have a Father who has good plans for you.

Did you know your Father has never stopped loving you?
Read Jeremiah 31:3
You have a Father whose love is steadfast.

Did you know the Father loves you so much
He sent His Son so you might know His love?
Read John 3:16
You have a Father who gave His all to have a relationship with you.

Did you know your Father wants your heart
to know an unexplainable love?
Read Ephesians 3:19
*You have a Father whose love will fill
every nook and cranny of your life.*

Did you know your Father loves you so much
He wants to make Himself at home in your life?
Read John 14:23
You have a Father who wants to be as close as He can.

Did you know your Father has never been ashamed of you?
Read Hebrews 11:16
You have a Father who is proud of you.

Did you know your Father will take a stand on your behalf?
Read Romans 8:31
You have a Father who is always for you.

Did you know your Father has forgiven you
and will never bring up your past?
Read Jeremiah 31:34
You have a Father who has chosen to remember your sin no more.

Did you know when you make a mistake,
your Father has an open-door policy?
Read 1 John 1:9
*You have a Father who never turns His
back on you when you're in trouble.*

Did you know your Father wants to use
you as an example of His love toward others?
Read 2 Corinthians 5:18
You have a Father who wants you to lead others to His love.

Did you know the Father's love will protect you?
Read 1 John 5:18
You have a Father who wants to keep you from harm.

Did you know your Father's love empowers you?
Read 2 Timothy 1:7
You have a Father whose love will equip you for living.

Did you know your Father will never leave
you and wants to meet all of your needs?
Read Luke 15:31
You have a Father who has provided everything you'll ever need.

A Family of Orphans

Although I loved and respected my dad, we never had a close relationship. I blame much of that on the Orphan Heart.

Out of eight siblings, Dad was the oldest boy. He had just turned twenty-two when his father died of appendicitis. Dad had to take over his dad's responsibilities for his mom and siblings. He paid all the bills and made sure everyone got an education. He took care of his mother until her death many years later. All of this left him bitter and angry.

Growing up, I never perceived that my dad loved me. Remember? The enemy loves to keep us away from our father's love. Dad took care of me and gave me three meals a day, clothes, and a roof over my head.

We went on family vacations together. In terms of material things, he was a good father, but I wanted to feel secure in him. Children get their identity from their fathers, so I kept looking to him for validation.

Looking back, I realize I spent much of my life trying to earn his love. Like the elder brother, I tried to be the perfect child. From cleaning up his shop to calling him about my professional achievements, I kept working to earn his approval. For my whole life, I was waiting to hear him say, "This is my son in whom I'm well-pleased."

During my father's last days, I was still waiting to hear it. For months, Dad was in and out of the hospital. One afternoon, the doctor told him, "This is the last time you get to speak to your sons. What do you want to say to them?"

"I've got nothing to say to those boys."

This closing statement made dad's death even more difficult. We wanted to grieve, but we were angry because Dad never said what we wanted to hear. In fact, I stayed angry—at God and at my dad—for many years. Satan used the hurts in my relationship with my Dad to drive the Orphan Heart deeper into my life.

Because I was an orphan, I produced orphans myself. An orphan can't produce people with sonship. Both my sons became orphans. Jeremiah grew up as the perfect child, and Caleb became the rebellious one. As soon as he graduated from high school, he ran away to California. He kept telling us he was going to make it big, but he only got deeper into all the things that pulled him away from God. Before long, he was eating from the West Coast version of a hog trough, out of money, and eager to come home.

Even after he returned to Tulsa, though, Caleb continued in his rebellious lifestyle. We never knew when we would see him, where he might be working, or what he might be doing. Until one day when he showed up at our door with a fresh tattoo, alcohol on his breath, and a teary confession: "Father, I have sinned against you. I come to ask forgiveness and submit myself to your authority again."

This was the first step in Caleb's long road back to our family and to the Father. But God had more work to do.

Our oldest son, Jeremiah, was the perfect child, the one who did everything right. At school, he took the accelerated classes. He planned his own budget and managed his money well. I thought everything was great with Jeremiah—until the day I cut down the tree.

"Vrrooom! Vroooom!" I stood out in our front yard revving my chain saw. Nothing makes a man feel more like a man than letting the whole neighborhood hear the sound of that motor. "Vroooooom! Vroooooom!" I revved it a few more times just in case someone missed it.

The cute little tree had stood beside our house for many years. But over time, it grew into a big problem. If I didn't cut it down, the experts said, it might crack our foundation. So there I stood, chain saw to the rescue.

As the branches and leaves fell, something else fell, too. White papers swirled around me as I hoisted the chainsaw high. I knew people used trees to make paper, but I never realized it could happen so fast.

I stopped the motor and glanced at one of the papers that came from the tree. "Jeremiah Moore" it said at the top. And a big red letter, "C."

I picked up another one. "Jeremiah Moore—D." And another "Jeremiah Moore—C-." He had stuffed all the papers with less-than-acceptable grades into a small hole in the tree outside his bedroom window. *Why would he do this?*

Right there, God spoke to my heart: *He didn't think his father would love him unless he was perfect.* I knew my children would remain orphans until I allowed God to change my Orphan Heart.

When my dad died without speaking worth and value into me, I thought I would remain in that angry, unfulfilled state forever. If there's anyone who should speak identity into your life this side of heaven, it should be your father. My father never did that for my brothers and me because no one had ever done it for him. And I passed my Orphan Heart right on down to my sons. But one night, God changed it all.

My Father's Favorite Child

About two years after Dad died, I spent the night in a hotel before speaking at a church in Chicago. The television had only two channels, and watching either one was like looking into a snowstorm. I lay on my bed and for some reason began reflecting on my relationship with my dad.

I knew I was preaching the next day on John 14, so I reread that chapter and kept going. When I came to John 17:23, I couldn't believe it. I didn't understand it, but I loved what it said—that God loves me as much as He loves His Son, Jesus. In fact, He sent Jesus to let me know of His love.

"You can't love me as much as You love Jesus," I told God. "He's the perfect child! Look at Him. He does everything right! Then look at me. I'm the broken child. I've done so many things wrong. Jesus is perfect. He must be your favorite child."

Again, God spoke to me. "What do you think you are?"

I didn't know how to answer that. *The terrible child? The messed-up child?*

But God said, "No. Based upon My Word, I want to tell you, if you call Jesus my favorite child, that makes you my favorite child, too."

For the first time, the thought entered my mind: *I am my Father's favorite child.* Of course, when that thought rose in my mind, all the negative ones, did, too: *You don't deserve to be the favorite. Why, just look at what you've done.*

But the truth of God is stronger than the biggest lie. What my earthly father could never do, my heavenly Father did. And that is the good news for every orphan. That weekend, on the outside, I was preaching, packing, and flying home. But on the inside, I was singing: *I am my Father's favorite child! I am my Father's favorite child!*

When I got home, I took my wife's lipstick (note: do not try this at home—unless you're willing to buy new lipstick) and wrote on our mirror: "I am my Father's favorite child." Once again, the enemy tried to bring thoughts to my mind that were contrary to the Word and will of God. But I kept embracing this truth and sharing it with everyone I knew. Before long, I was taking a mirror along with me when I preached. I can't tell you how many people wept as they looked into it and embraced the truth: *I am my Father's favorite child.*

No matter what my earthly father thought or thinks about me, no matter how many wounds I have from the past, no matter what I may or may not do in the future, I am my Father's favorite child. He loves me. And embracing that truth has made all the difference.

What difference will it make in you?

The Battle: Take a mirror and, using lipstick or nail polish, write, "I am my Father's favorite child" across its surface. Every morning and night this week, look at yourself in the mirror and read those words aloud. As you do so, you are speaking against the enemy's lies.

11—Renewed:

You don't have to live this way anymore.

"In Sugamo Prison, as he was told of Watanabe's fate, all Louie saw was a lost person, a life now beyond redemption. He felt something that he had never felt for his captor before. With a shiver of amazement, he realized that it was compassion.

At that moment, something shifted sweetly inside him. It was forgiveness, beautiful and effortless and complete. For Louie Zamperini, the war was over."—Laura Hillenbrand, *Unbroken*[1]

Elizabeth's Story

The Orphan Heart ties you to the past and keeps you from enjoying the future. That's so unbelievably true in my mom's life. The daughter of two parents with Orphan Hearts, she became an orphan, too. Although she chose to make sure her kids had a better life, she still struggles with acceptance. She had a million hurts as a child, and they've continued into her adult life.

It breaks my heart to see my mom so tied to the past. And my dad is an orphan who pours everything into his work. You know what Walker teaches about orphans producing orphans? That definitely happened to me.

I'll never forget the first time I heard him teach on the Orphan Heart. He had a mirror there, and no matter how long it took, you had to get up there and say it: "I am my Father's favorite child." I don't know just why, but I always wanted to be accepted. I always felt like the odd one out. My relationships were very shallow even though I wanted them to be very deep.

I still struggle in some areas, but not as much as before I knew the Orphan Heart teaching. I know that I am my Father's favorite child. When you know that, it's liberating. Not when you're just taught it for the first time, but when the Spirit moves in your life and you know that you know that you know because the Spirit of God is telling you.

There's a difference between reading and hearing this teaching. But unless you're prepared to accept it, there's no freedom, and you'll still be bound to your past. You have to work to be set free. You have to want to be your Father's favorite child. I think my mom thinks she's not worthy of that.

For me, when we had to say we were our Father's favorite child, I believed it. It was the real deal. ...I felt like I was living a new life, waking up with a fresh start on life once I knew that. But I remember it took a while. And it took a while for that room [where Walker gave the Orphan Heart teaching] to clear out. It took some of the students who got in front of the mirror several minutes to be able to say it. But you knew the Spirit was doing a work.

This generation is nothing but orphans. The divorce rate in our society is fifty percent or higher. We have kids who are having kids, and why is that? You can attribute most of it to the fact that they don't have two parents or are spiritual orphans.

We try to fill that void with so many different things. ...When you're an orphan and you don't have love, you try to find it in other people. ...The love that you lack, you will try to fill with whatever comes your way.

As a parent, I know orphans produce orphans, and I don't want that for my kids. It's one thing knowing this teaching before you're a parent, and it's another thing trying to live it out. I want my kids to know beyond the shadow of a doubt that I love them, but God loves them so much more than I do. We will fail them as parents, but God is never going to fail them.

Throughout this book, we have learned that the enemy wants to make us orphans, so he tells us the biggest lie: We don't matter. We don't have a Father who loves us.

But how does God want us to live? In the second chapter of Acts, we see a picture of the very first believers who came to know Christ after Peter's sermon at Pentecost. What kind of people did they become as they embraced the good news of the Gospel and moved into sonship? Here, God gives us a clue: "They were continually devoting themselves to the apostles' teaching and to fellowship, to the breaking of bread and to prayer. Everyone kept feeling a sense of awe; and many wonders and signs were taking place through the apostles" (Acts 2:42-43).

I read those verses for many years before I understood what the *awe* was all about. While still a youth minister, I began to seek the Lord and pray. What did God mean by the *awe?* And how could I get it?

Awestruck

At the time, I was serving at the largest Baptist church in Tulsa. I knew youth pastors were supposed to do three things with their students: evangelize them, disciple them, and take them to Six Flags somewhere in America. And it was about time for our students' annual trip to the Six Flags in Arlington, Texas.

We had a young man in our youth group named Charles. Charles was mentally handicapped. He enjoyed Sunday School class, but he couldn't do most of the things the other students did. But God placed Charles on my heart. Deep down inside, I knew he needed this trip.

One evening, I made a visit to his parents. "Would you please let Charles go with us?" I begged. "I'll watch over him. I'll be his room-mate and ride every ride with him. Won't you please let him go?"

They gave their permission, and at 4 a.m. the next Saturday morning, the bus pulled out of the church parking lot. After the four-hour drive to Six Flags, I blinked, looked up, and thought the Rapture had taken place. Everyone had left the bus to ride the rides, eat the snacks, and have a wonderful time at Six Flags.

Everyone except Charles, rocking back and forth, back and forth in the seat behind me. "Come on, Charles," I told him. "Let's go!"

I grabbed his hand, planning to head for the Kiddy section and show him a good time. We passed a ride with small boats that floated into a cave where puppet-like figures waved at all the boat riders. *This looks like something Charles can handle.*

Before long, Charles and I were floating through the cave. We'd only been inside twenty or thirty seconds when he began to cry, softly at first, then louder. "Charles, Charles, what's wrong? Are you scared?"

"N-n-n-no," he choked out. "Walker, I wanna ride the Texas Cliffhanger!" His sobs grew even louder. "I wanna ride the Texas Cliffhanger!"

"Charles! Quit your crying and we'll ride it!"

I had no idea what the Texas Cliffhanger was, but if the promise of a ride would keep Charles quiet, we'd go. Even in the darkness, I could feel people staring. I didn't want to travel the rest of the way with my ride partner's screams echoing through the cave.

Finally, our boat landed, and we began looking for the ride Charles wanted to try. Finally, I saw what had to be the longest line in the entire park. Right next to it stood a sign that read "The Texas Cliffhanger."

Charles and I got in line and traveled back and forth for what seemed like hours. I kept seeing the same little faces staring at me as we worked our way through. Finally, we reached the front of the line, and I saw the ride we'd waited so long to reach. A small wire cage with three plastic seats inside simulated what passengers would experience in an elevator that freefell for ten stories. Oh, and did I mention I have a fear of heights?

As we stood there watching the last few people in front of us, I memorized everything Charles and I were about to experience. When we sat down, the operator would fasten a bar across our waists as two more bars came down across our shoulders. The cage would ascend, click-click-click-click, ten stories into the sky where it would push out on a track. Next, the ride would beep three times. On the third beep, a metal pin would pull, and the cage would freefall for ten stories, faster and faster. As it reached the bottom, the track would curve up so we'd end up on our backs for a few seconds. Finally, it would shift again so we'd finish in an upright position.

I turned to Charles for one last plea. "Charles, are you *sure* you want to ride this ride?"

"Yes, Brother Walker. I wanna ride the ride! I wanna ride the ride!"

At this point, I wasn't sure who was more handicapped: Charles or I. I knew better than to get on that ride, and yet I planned to do it anyway—all because of my foolish promise.

Our turn. We entered the wire cage and sat in the plastic seats. The attendant snapped the bar across our waists as the other bars came down over our shoulders. We began going up, click-click-click-click. And I said a prayer I often pray: "Lord Jesus, come quickly. Lord Jesus, come quickly."

I didn't have to look over at Charles because I could hear him screaming, "Wheee!" He was having a wonderful time.

We got to the top, and the cage pushed out on the track. I knew what would happen next. The ride beeped once. It beeped twice. And on the third beep, God spoke: "Walker, *this* is the awe."

In that one nanosecond, I was never so scared and so excited in all my life. The mixture of tremendous fear and incredible excitement colliding in a single moment is what Scripture calls the *awe*.

We saw the awe in the disciples' lives, too. They followed Jesus up to His crucifixion, when fear filled their hearts. But when He rose from the grave on the third day, and they were able to walk and talk with Him again, their excitement rose. After He ascended to heaven, they were again lost and confused, "like sheep without a shepherd" (Mark 6:34).

But in the second chapter of Acts, God sent the Holy Spirit as a mighty rushing wind and tongues of fire. Peter went out to the marketplace to speak, and 3000 came to faith in Christ. The message of Jesus was transforming people's lives and setting them free. The masses were receiving eternal life. All at once, the disciples were scared to death and incredibly excited. Just like me, waiting for the pin to pull at the top of the Texas Cliffhanger, they were in awe.

The Word

God never designed us to live as orphans. The Orphan Heart is totally out of our nature. He created us to be an awe-some people who live, dwell, and abide in the awe of God.

The enemy does not want us to have that close fellowship with the Father. He doesn't want us to walk out the destiny God created us to fulfill. And he uses the lies of the entire world to keep us from understanding the joy of being the Father's favorite child.

God has given us a plan, a way for us to leave the Orphan Heart, to move into sonship and experience the awe. I call the elements of this plan the *awe factors*. Let's explore them, one at a time.

In the first part of Acts 2:42, Luke tells us the believers were "continually devoting themselves to the apostles' teaching." Jesus told the

Jews who believed in Him, "If you continue in My Word, *then* you are truly disciples of mine; and you will know the truth, and the truth will make you free" (John 8:31-32). That's why we must get into His Word and apply it to every one of the orphan lies the enemy sends our way.

How can the Word of God help an orphan? Think back to the temptation of Jesus. Every time Satan came to Him, He offered the Word in response. And by replacing the enemy's lies with God's truth as found in His Word, we can drive out the Orphan Heart.

God says His Word has a specific purpose in our lives: "All Scripture is inspired by God and profitable for teaching for reproof, for correction, for training in righteousness" (2 Tim. 3:16). The training of the Word helps us understand the difference between lies and truth. We can compare it to a ruler that we hold against everything we hear. If a statement or voice in our head doesn't line up, it's a lie. If it's a truth from God, it will build us, grow us, and make us more profitable. Jesus emphasized, "If you abide in Me, and My words abide in you, ask whatever you wish, and it will be done for you" (John 15:7).

Make Yourself at Home

Scripture also tells us, "For this reason we also constantly thank God that when you received the word of God which you heard from us, you accepted *it* not as the word of men, but *for* what it really is, the word of God, which also performs its work in you who believe" (1 Thess. 2:13). God's Word is proactive. It's always at work. And we change as we receive it, as we allow it to make itself at home (another translation of the word for *abide* in John 15:7) in our lives.

But what does "make itself at home" mean? I started pondering this when some friends invited me over for dinner several years ago. "Make yourself at home," they told me, leaving me in their living room as they stepped into the kitchen to put the final touches on our dinner.

The first thing I did was look around. I noticed the comfortable couch, the crowded bookshelves, and the gilded antique clock standing tall in one corner. "Make yourself at home," my friends had said. But what did they mean?

As I pondered this thought, I spied a few books on a nearby shelf that stuck out several inches past the others. I jumped up to find a more suitable place for the misfits and settle myself back on the couch again.

I'll admit it. I've logged just enough hours on HG-TV to be dangerous. Once I sat down, I couldn't help but see a painting someone must have bumped. When I got up to straighten it, I realized a lamp blocked its view, so I moved the offending light fixture to the other side of the room.

"Make yourself at home!" My hosts' thoughtful words echoed in my mind.

"If this were really my home, I'd move this chair here, and put this one over there." I was tugging the final piece of furniture into position when my friends reappeared.

"Dinner's ready," they chorused as confusion crossed their faces.

"What were you doing, Walker?" the wife asked.

"Umm, just what you said. I was making myself at home," I beamed. What a wonderful visit this was turning out to be!

When we give God's Word the freedom to make itself at home in our lives, we give it the same freedom I took in rearranging my friends' living room. The Word can shift our spirits. It can readjust our souls. It can even move our attitudes from one place to another. And by the time it gets done, nothing will ever be the same.

Fellowship: Caleb, the Kindergarten Witness

But staying in God's Word isn't the only way we remain in the awe of God. The second awe factor, or element in which the first believer continued, is *fellowship*. When we use that word today, it usually has some connection with food: church fellowship (a social event where we eat), fellowship hall (the place at the church where, again, we eat), fellowship meal (connecting fellowship with food once again). But to a true believer, fellowship is much more than food.

By now, I'm sure you know why I call my son Caleb my "special" child. From his earliest days, he's had the gift of being in the center of something unusual. On his first day of kindergarten, his teacher recognized it, too. She and her new students were getting to know each other when she looked out over the class and saw my blonde, blue-eyed son with his hand held high.

"Yes, Caleb, what do you want?"

"Do you know Jesus Christ as your Lord and Savior?" came the little voice.

"Caleb, you can't ask that question in school. Now, let's get back to learning about our class job chart."

Ten minutes of kindergarten activity passed. But Caleb couldn't keep quiet for long. He raised his hand again.

"Yes, Caleb?" The teacher didn't sound quite so patient this time.

"You know if you don't, you're going to hell."

I heard this story an hour or two later, when the principal called me to come to his office. Here I was, a grown man, sitting in the place I most tried to avoid as a student—and on my son's first day of school.

"Your son talked about Jesus. I appreciate his concern for his teacher, but that doesn't reflect the values of our school system."

But I knew something the principal didn't know. As the birds fly in the air and as the fish swim in the sea, talking about Jesus is the most natural thing for believers. All Caleb was doing was what the Father created him to do. As Christ-followers, we have the responsibility to surround ourselves with people who will speak to us the language of God's Word.

If we have a relationship with God and remain in the same community that made us an orphan, we'll hear things contrary to His Word and will that only serve to drive the Orphan Heart deeper into our lives. Sometimes we may not be able to leave that community. No matter what, we must surround ourselves with a group of believers who will build us up and speak truth into our lives. They'll make what I call *grace deposits* into our spiritual bank accounts by speaking words that affirm and build us up.

True fellowship helps us walk in sonship and drive away the Orphan Heart. And that's something you can't get from a potluck meal.

Praise and Worship: Lesson from the Amish

I grew up in a small country church, where we only had a pastor and no other staff. The guy who led the worship was a farmer. I don't think he could read notes or even knew much about music—he just liked to wave his arms. We didn't even have a choir. Almost everything I knew about worship came from a group called the Wildwood Quartet, who came and sang at our church every once in a while.

I think that's why I have a harder time with this awe factor than the others. The rest of what I learned about praise and worship came not from my church but from the nearby Amish community. It wasn't unusual for us to see Amish people in their simple dress or Amish horses and buggies going down the road. But what everyone went to the

Amish for was their food and their furniture. People would drive a long way to get either one.

One day, I went with my mom to buy some bread from the Amish store. We waited in line behind a man. When he got to the counter, the Amish woman asked what he wanted.

"I hope you baked me some bread," he told her in a hearty voice.

She answered in a soft voice, "We didn't bake any for you. We baked our bread for Jesus, but you can have some."

In the Amish community, everything is considered an act of worship. As 1 Corinthians 10:31 says, "Whether then, you eat or drink or whatever you do, do all to the glory of God." Every loaf of bread, every pie, every pan of rolls or piece of furniture that the Amish make, they do for Jesus. And even though I'm not Amish, I understand that everything I do is an act of worship to Him.

Prayer: Red Sea or Gethsemane?

The final element that marked the lives of the new believers in Acts 2—and our lives as we move away from the Orphan Heart—is prayer. Many people fail to see the full value of prayer. But once we understand it from the Father's perspective, we realize it's all about our relationship with Him. At that point, we understand the meaning of Romans 8:28, which says, "And we know that God causes all things to work together for good to those who love God, to those who are called according to *His* purpose."

That small country church my family attended? You've seen dozens just like it. This white frame building was surrounded by a cemetery. I guess the congregation wanted to be as close as possible to the resurrection of the dead.

The thing I remember most about the church, though, was not its cemetery, but its prayer life. These people prayed all the time. I don't mean the type of prayer meetings we see in our churches today, but an entire congregation broken and weeping as people took their requests before the Lord.

This thing called prayer has always confused me. Sometimes I pray, and God moves heaven and earth on my behalf. At other times prayer feels as though I'm tossing bricks skyward. Many of us have prayed for years without feeling as though God hears us.

Some time ago, God began teaching me that our prayers end up in one of two places. The first is the Red Sea. Think back to Exodus 14, when Moses was bringing the Israelites out of the Promised Land. There in the wilderness, he encountered what seemed like an insurmountable problem. The Israelite people, who must have been the ancestors of today's church members, whined and complained. "We would have been better off if Moses had left us to die," they said. "We want to go back to Egypt!"

Moses, already a wise leader, told his crabby crew to wait and see what great things God would do. And you know the rest of the story. God parted the Red Sea so Moses and his band of renown could cross in safety.

Red Sea prayers end with God changing the external. As a missionary, I've often witnessed the results of prayers like these. For example, our ministry has never asked for money. Instead, we pray and leave our requests at God's doorstep. One day we needed $5,000 to meet an urgent need. My wife and I were in the back of our office praying when we heard someone yelling, "I'm a delivery boy from God!"

We ran to the front to check out the commotion, and there on the ground lay a plain, unmarked envelope. We opened it and found the exact amount of money we needed. Our prayers ended in the Red Sea, where God moved external circumstances to meet our needs.

But not all prayers are answered this way. When his son became ill, King David didn't get the answer he wanted. For seven days he prayed and asked God to heal the infant boy, but his son died anyway. And when Paul asked God to remove the thorn in his flesh, He didn't do that, either.

Even Jesus, in Matthew 26, asked God if it would be possible to remove the cross. This is the only time in Scripture we see Jesus repeat a prayer. Three times, He asked His Heavenly Father if He had another plan. But God didn't offer one.

All these prayers ended up not in the Red Sea but in Gethsemane. A Red Sea prayer changes external circumstances. But a Gethsemane prayer changes *us*. Instead of changing the external, it changes the internal.

A Gethsemane prayer changed King David. He rose from his prayer to worship God. A Gethsemane prayer also changed Paul. He realized the thorn in his flesh was meant to keep him humble. And of course, a Gethsemane prayer changed Jesus. Each time He prayed, He moved from "Let this cup pass from Me" to "Your kingdom come. Your will be done."

All prayers end in one of two places: the Red Sea, where God does an incredible thing and changes the external; or Gethsemane, where He changes the internal. Jesus says in Luke 9:23 that we must deny ourselves, take up our cross daily, and follow Him. Unless you pass through Gethsemane, you can't reach the cross.

Which is the greater prayer: Red Sea or Gethsemane? I believe the Gethsemane prayer has more power because a changed life changes lives.

Our prayers begin with surrender when we go to our knees. But they also end with surrender when we tell our heavenly Father, "Your will be done."

When I pray, I don't know whether God will take my prayer to the Red Sea, where I can stand by and watch His glory; or to Gethsemane, where His glory is revealed in me. But I do know what I desire most: Your kingdom come, Your will be done. And as long as He is with us, He can take our prayers—and us—wherever He thinks best.

Whether our prayers go to the Red Sea or to Gethsemane, we know God is using them to move us toward the destiny He has for us and to make us an effective part of the body of Christ. Like the believers in Acts 2:43, when we have all the awe factors, we experience "a sense of awe." And as we work out our salvation, awe becomes a lifestyle. We live without guilt because we're not tied to the past. We live without worry because we're not tied to the future. And we escape the lie because we are released from the bondage of the Orphan Heart and can truly say we are free indeed.

The Battle: Worship makes us stronger and equips us to fight the lies of the enemy. Today, listen to one or more praise songs and (if possible) sing along. Watch for other ways you can worship as you move through your day.

12—Restored:

You matter to God; you matter to me.

"I hated the dismal place full of sick and suffering women, but we had to go back, again and again, for Betsie's condition was growing worse. She was not repelled by the room as I was. To her it was simply a setting in which to talk about Jesus—as indeed was everyplace else. Wherever she was, at work, in the food line, in the dormitory, Betsie spoke to those around her about His nearness and His yearning to come into their lives. As her body grew weaker, her faith seemed to grow bolder. And sick call was 'such an important place, Corrie! Some of these people are at the very threshold of heaven!'"—Corrie ten Boom with John and Elizabeth Sherrill, *The Hiding Place*[1]

Penny's Story (from a letter sent to Walker Moore)

I was orphaned as a child. My mother died when I was five years old, and I never knew my father. My grandparents raised me. I experienced horrible abuse in several ways: verbal, sexual, etc. I was always seeking the love I needed.

As a teenager, I made some very poor choices. I was told all my growing years that I was worthless and that no one would love someone like me. I became a child of God at church camp the summer I turned seventeen.

I still needed that love and sense of belonging and self-worth with my earthly grandparents, but it never happened. When my grandmother was on her death-

bed, more than anything else, I wanted her to say she loved me. But she didn't have the love of God in her heart.

"I love you," I told her.

She looked at me and said, "What are you waiting for?"

I turned and walked away, and she passed without ever telling me she loved me.

I was at church Sunday morning and sat in the front row. I did not come Sunday night, but listened to your message on my church's website. I took notes as I listened.

As I heard your story about your father, I began to weep. I am my heavenly Father's favorite child! I have my identity. God loves me equally as Jesus. I have worth and value.

"Our heavenly Father speaks into us our identity." I got down on my knees and thanked my Father God for speaking into me my identity. My life has new meaning and I will never be the same.

From the beginning, God created us for a purpose. He designed us to be reflectors or mirrors of His life and love. But the biggest lie shattered the mirror. The more we believe we don't matter to God, that He doesn't love us and care for us, the deeper the lie takes root, and the bigger orphans we become.

In Matthew 5:13, Jesus tells us, "You are the salt of the earth; but if the salt has become tasteless, how can it be made salty *again*? It is no longer good for anything, except to be thrown out and trampled under foot by men." This whole book is about how to get back to being salt, being someone who makes a difference. Being someone who experiences the awe once again.

Love One Another

In order for us to fully reflect Him, God calls us to do two things. First, He calls us to love one another. In fact, He does more than call us; He commands us (John 13:34-35).

My time in the military taught me about commands. Our drill sergeants barked orders all day long: "Fall in!" "About face!" "Forward, march!" From the time I got up until the time I went to bed, I spent my days responding to commands.

The fact that Jesus made these words a commandment means we should have no question about what He wants for our lives. He intends us to love others as He loves us. But loving others is one of the things someone with an Orphan Heart can't do. An orphan doesn't have the capacity to love the way Jesus does. He loves us with the love of the Father who taught Him to love. There is no greater love story than the one between Jesus and His Father, who demonstrated this love in giving it to us (Rom. 5:8).

And yet there is no greater demonstration of people *not* loving one another than within the body of Christ. How many churches have started because of a split? We make jokes about high attendance at church business meetings because everyone shows up for the fight. So many people go to hockey games waiting for the fight to break out. And far too many people go to church for the same thing.

The only way we can love as Jesus loved is to accept and embrace the Father's love. We can't love out of a vacuum. We can't reach into nothing and say, "Look what I have to give." Only when you are filled with the love of the Father can you extend that love to others.

The Overflow

When I was in college, I had a professor named Dr. Burns. He was the strict type of teacher, always serious. And I had the double blessing of having him as my advisor. I may as well have had course planning sessions with Attila the Hun.

Dr. Burns was a master at saying things that would motivate me to work hard without me realizing what he was doing. If I said, "I'm going to preach student revivals," he would shoot back with, "That'll never happen." And before I knew it, I found myself calling around to various churches, seeing how many of them would schedule me to preach their next series of youth meetings.

I always set out to prove him wrong. In one class, I had to preach, and I knew he would grade my message. I came up with the best sermon since the day of Pentecost. I preached, I spit, I did all the right hand motions. Everything I did, I did to impress Dr. Burns. I knew he'd have to give me an A-plus. Either that, or the Holy Spirit didn't live in him, and he was lost.

He flunked me.

I went in to see him as soon as I could. There had to be a mistake. Was there a missing leg on that *A?*

"That was a good message," Dr. Burns said, leaning back in his office chair. He looked at me over the tops of his glasses. "But you either preach from your mind or your heart. You need to have so much in you that when someone jostles you, it splashes out on them. You were preaching to please your audience, son, but you weren't preaching from your heart."

That's what Jesus was talking about in John 13:34-35. Love is like the best kind of sermon. It's something that happens out of the overflow of our relationship with God. It's not something we manufacture, work at, strive to do, or obtain. True love comes from the overflow of a loving relationship with our living, loving Father.

Being in ministry as long as I have, people will come up to me and say things like, "Mrs. So-and-so has been gossiping about me again, but I'm trying to love her with the love of Jesus." They don't get it. You don't try. You *are* the love of the Father in you. When we're living and dwelling in Him, He can't help but flow out of our lives.

So many people try to attain this love. It's the same perfect love 1 Corinthians 13 describes in such a beautiful way. But we can't act or be a certain way in order to reach it. Love comes from relationship. It flows out of knowing our identity, purpose, direction, and destiny. It flows from abundant life. The love we extend to others begins with our love for a holy God.

When we have this love, we become salt and light. We start affecting others around us. We quit doing and start being.

So if someone tries to work up the love of God or manufacture it, he fails—because it has to come from the overflow. No sonship, no overflow. No sonship, no awe. No sonship, no life. The enemy thinks he can keep us from being centered in the awe of God, where the past is forgiven and the future is covered. But we can live in the moment. We can live in the awe of God. When we have freedom from the Orphan Heart, we are free to love others as our Father loves us. And that means we are free indeed.

Too Difficult to Replicate

Did you know there is an entire industry built on the making, recording, and breaking of records? I'm not talking about the vinyl discs that used to hold our music. I'm talking about the kind of record that appears in the famous *Guinness Book.*

I learned much more about records this year. When my team and I carried a cross to the top of Tanzania's Mount Kilimanjaro, we didn't know it, but we set a world record. No one ever took a cross that high (19,341 feet to the summit) before.

I first learned of our accidental achievement when the good people at Guinness got in touch with me, mentioned the record, and asked me to provide verification of the climb.

Verification? My grandfather taught me a man's word was his bond. But as it turns out, the Guinness people have some very specific requirements. I had to provide photographs, newspaper documentation, signatures, and other proof that we'd done what we said we did.

But you won't find my name or a picture of our team in the 2014 edition of the *Guinness Book*. After I submitted all the documentation, my *Guinness* friends sent me another letter:

> Dear Walker,
> Unfortunately, what you have achieved with your team, al-
> beit an excellent feat, cannot be recognized by Guinness
> World Records because it would be too difficult to repli-
> cate. . . .
> Thank you and we hope you understand.
> Yours sincerely,
> Johanna Hessling
> Guinness World Records

"Too difficult to replicate?" I didn't understand. I thought that was the whole point of a world's record: to perform a feat so stupendous, so outstanding that few people could hope to repeat it. People enjoy seeing the biggest, the best, and the greatest. But apparently taking a cross to the summit of Mount Kilimanjaro wasn't quite it.

People were looking for the greatest back in Jesus' time, too. In fact, Matthew records that the Pharisees came to Jesus and asked, "Teacher, which is the greatest commandment in the law?" (Matt. 22:36). Even back then, people wanted to identify the biggest and the best.

Jesus told them the greatest commandment was not one but two things: loving God and loving people. And those are two things orphans can't do. First, orphans can't love God. They can't accept Him as a loving Father. And if they can't do that, of course they have no overflow that allows them to love other people.

Into All the World

Jesus gave His disciples the Great Commandment (Mark 12:30-31) before He gave the Great Commission in Matthew 28:18-20. Do you find it ironic that He would tell us to love God and our neighbors with all our being before He told us to go into all the world (Mark 16:15)? Do you find it ironic that, later in the Bible, He devotes an entire book (1 John) to the topic of love?

Of course not, because love is the essence of everything. Sharing our faith is a part of loving people out of the overflow of God's love for us. But since our churches are full of orphans who can't do the Great Commandment, we have to figure out ways to motivate people to share their faith. Most outreach programs in our churches can be described as safari hunts into Lost-land.

The typical outreach program works like this: all the hunters gather together on Monday night with a list of the people we're praying for. We pray to the Big Hunter in the sky. Then, we go into Lost-land and, when someone accepts Christ, we act as though we bagged one: "We got this sinner today! We led him to Christ."

If our churches don't participate in game hunts, they try to get us to herd the fish into the big stained-glass aquarium on Sunday mornings.

The Reverend Doctor Pastor throws out his fishing hooks on Sunday morning. All of a sudden, he catches one and hauls it, flopping, down the aisle. We all stand and applaud because the professional fisherman has done it again.

But those game hunts and fishing expeditions are so contrary to Scripture. Instead, God wants us to be free from the past, free from the future, and free to live in the awe of God. Out of this relationship, we can love the unlovable. Out of this relationship, we can pray for the one who spitefully uses us. Out of this relationship, we can go into all the world. And we don't see any of these things as rules or commandments. Instead, we see them as opportunities to bring great joy to our Father.

Jesus says, "If you love me, you will keep My commandments" (John 14:15). Love is the hallmark of our relationship with Him. We love Him not out of obligation but out of relationship. An orphan, however, does everything out of obligation. (See Appendix 1, "You Might Have an Orphan Heart If. . .")

I travel our country and preach in all sorts of churches. I can try to convince them of the need to go and tell. I can show pictures of starving children in Ethiopia or old men bowing to Buddha in China. I can tell of the great lostness of our world, and that places exist where no one has ever heard the gospel. The people will applaud and give me money to go.

But it doesn't work that way. The enemy sits to the side, a smug look on his face, knowing he's done the one thing that keeps our whole world from knowing the love of the Father. If he keeps us from knowing our Father's love, He keeps us from loving others. If he keeps us from loving others, he keeps us from telling them about Jesus. And if he keeps us from loving others, he keeps us far away from the abundant life.

Orphan on a Mission

I'll never forget the year Darlene served with us as part of our student leadership. What we didn't realize until too late was that Darlene had an Orphan Heart.

When orphans go to the mission field, they work to change the agenda from reaching others with the gospel (fulfilling the Great Commission) to taking care of themselves. Darlene had served in the same country the year before, so she had some insights into the area. One by one, she went to all the students on the team and began to subtly shift their loyalties from our Country Coordinators (head leaders) to herself.

"I don't think that's the best choice," she would say about a decision our Country Coordinators made. "They don't know what they're doing." Her special knowledge allowed her to cast doubt into the students' minds before anyone realized how the enemy was using her.

On that trip, our team members were staying in church members' homes. Because Darlene already knew the host missionaries, it was easy for her to convince them to let her stay with them. She used the extra time in their home to make more divisive remarks. And before long, her words built a wall between the missionaries and our Country Coordinators.

In the end, this young woman succeeded in turning our team's focus from outward (the people of the nation they served) to inward (each other). Everywhere she went, she created chaos that made it hard for the team to minister effectively.

But why would an orphan go to the mission field in the first place? To hide an Orphan Heart. Remember, orphans often want to give the appearance of doing right (the "perfect" child). But then they have to create all sorts of distractions to avoid doing what they can't do anyway.

That summer, God still used our team. But He did it in spite of, not because of, Darlene. As an orphan, she couldn't fulfill the Great Commandment by loving God and loving other people. And when it came to fulfilling the Great Commission, she couldn't do that either. She couldn't spread the love she didn't have. The only thing she could share was her Orphan Heart.

Saving Mr. Banks

Anyone who has seen the movie *Saving Mr. Banks* can tell right away that *Mary Poppins* author Pamela Travers, played by actress Emma Stone, is a disturbed woman. Walt Disney, played by Tom Hanks, found that out. Hoping to keep a promise he made to his two little girls, he waited for the movie rights to her book for almost twenty years. When Travers finally came to America to help work on the script, her overbearing attitude and snippy remarks caused problems for almost everyone.

But those who understand the Orphan Heart have special insight into the character of Pamela Travers. As the movie progresses, it becomes clear that for Pamela, Mr. Banks (the banker who hires Mary Poppins to care for his children) is Travers Goff, her father. The book, and later the movie, represent her attempts to do what she could never do in real life: please him. She wanted to please him so much, in fact, that instead of using her real name, Helen Goff, she took on a false identity, Pamela Travers, using her father's first name as her last.

Does any of this sound familiar? Let's look at the downward spiral of the Orphan Heart in Helen Goff's life.

Although she loved him, Helen's father, an alcoholic, rejected her, then died when she was only ten years old. *No father, no identity.*

Her father's rejection caused Helen to question her ability as a writer. *No identity, no purpose.*

For twenty years, Helen refused to allow Disney to purchase the rights to *Mary Poppins* and only granted them as a last resort. *No purpose, no direction.*

Even while the movie was being made, Helen's focus remained on preserving her father's image, thus "saving Mr. Banks" rather than the millions of children who would watch the film. *No direction, no destiny.*

Near the end of the film, Walt Disney reveals that he, too, had a demanding father and urges Helen to find freedom in a life not controlled by the past. She disagrees. *No destiny, no life.*

Out of Focus

You see, my missionary friend Darlene and Pamela Travers/Helen Goff shared the same problem. Because they were both victims of the Orphan Heart, they both had the wrong focus. And that wrong focus caused them to miss the joyful, abundant, overflowing lives God intended them to have.

As I was finishing this book, I gained some insights into what it's like to have the wrong focus. I was in Mexico with a group of students doing mission work. Forty-nine of us were jammed together in a church, living, eating, and serving God together.

The difference between my age and the students' is getting increasingly wide. One of them asked me how old I was, and I told her.

"Wow! You're older than my grandparents!" she said, then caught herself. "Oh! But you look and act younger than they do." Good try, but a little late.

I realize I'm not as young as I used to be. The eye doctor tells me I have the beginning of cataracts, and the gleam in my eyes now comes from the sun hitting my bifocals. When I see a quarter on the floor, it's not worth the effort to bend over and pick it up. My wife complains that I keep the volume on the television uncomfortably loud. But I'm not sure how she knows. She's getting as deaf as I am.

Still, I don't mind getting older. I've learned there are a number of perks. Your supply of brain cells is finally down to a manageable size. You secrets are safe with your friends because they can't remember them either. You can sing along with elevator music. You don't need a twenty-year guarantee for the things you buy. Your joints are more accurate at predicting the weather than the local meteorologist. And there is nothing left to learn the hard way.

But one morning, I had a scare. I got up at six o'clock to do my quiet time, reading my Bible and meditating upon its meaning. I didn't want to disturb the students, so I reached over in the dark, put on my glasses, and opened up my Kindle Fire to read the Scriptures. Sometimes my eyes take a few minutes to adjust first thing in the morning. But today, nothing looked right. I squinted, hoping that would help, but the blurriness only got worse.

I held the Kindle farther away from my face. Sometimes that fixes the problem, but this time, it didn't work. I finally adjusted the font size to the largest setting, the size of a Volkswagen Beetle. It was so large someone a few blocks away could read it. But even at that size, the type was blurry. I kept reading, figuring sooner or later my sight would snap back into focus. I spent an hour trying to make out the big fuzzy letters. When my eyes got too tired, I lay back down on my cot, covered my eyes with my arm, and started praying.

There are several kinds of prayers. There's the one that comes off the top of your head when you're asked to bless the meal at Uncle Albert's house, and then there's the one that comes from somewhere deep inside as you cry out to God. This prayer was the latter. I needed

God to heal my eyes. How could I make it through the day or even drive our team where they needed to go if everything was out of focus? I had lain there for some time praying when I heard one of our leaders ask, "Has anybody seen my glasses?"

A thought popped into my mind. *Could it be?*

Interrupting one of the greatest-ever prayers for healing, I slowly raised my arm and pulled off my glasses. Upon close examination, I realized the truth. Somehow in the darkness, I had reached over and picked up the wrong pair. I gave them back, put on my own glasses, and my focus was restored.

But I'm not the only who has the wrong focus. The biggest lie—the lie that says you don't matter to God—takes our focus off our living, loving Lord and puts it on ourselves. Our guilt and shame tie us to the past. Our worry ties us to the future. We spend our lives hiding, doing our best to look as though we have it all together on the outside when we're dying on the inside.

None of this is the abundant life Jesus promised us. None of this is walking in sonship or experiencing the awe. And none of this is what He wants for our lives.

When He told us, "I will not leave you as orphans, I will come to you" (John 14:18), He wasn't just talking about His return. When we confess our Orphan Hearts and call on Him as our loving Father, He will come to us. He will make Himself at home in our lives and rearrange them as we spend time in His Word. He will warm us with fellowship of our fellow believers. He will change things—or change us—as we further our relationship with Him in prayer. And He will bless us as we worship Him in spirit and truth.

Throughout our time together, I've told lots of stories: stories from the Bible, stories from the mission field, and stories from my own life and those of people I know. Think through some of these stories. Re-visit the "You Might Have an Orphan Heart If. . ." Chart at the end of this book. And ask God to show you if—no matter how long you've known and served Him—you need to escape the lie.

For you see, your story has yet to be written. Why not allow Him to write it with the identity, purpose, direction, destiny, and life He has planned for you? After all, He loves you as much as He loves His Son Jesus. You're His favorite child.

He will not leave you as an orphan. He will come to you.

The Battle: Has God used this book to reveal any element of the Orphan Heart in your life? If so, confess this to God and ask His help in walking in the abundant life true sonship brings.

You might have an Orphan Heart if...

Little things bother you.

When in a room of people, you always feel small.

You feel jealous when others receive recognition.

What you do never seems to be good enough.

You've asked God multiple times to forgive you of a specific sin.

You often say to yourself, "I've got to do better next time."

If you don't get to buy something new, you feel miserable.

You sacrifice providing for your needs to take care of your wants.

You use people instead of serving them.

Your first response is anger.

You're driven to outperform everyone else.

You feel as though everyone's efforts get recognized except yours.

You're always the bridesmaid, never the bride.

You look in the mirror and criticize yourself.

At night, you have trouble turning off your thoughts.

You can't pass a mirror without stopping and evaluating yourself.

You can forgive everyone but yourself.

You have constant, nagging thoughts of insecurity.

You wish you were someone else.

You turn to food, alcohol, or other pleasures when stressed.

You know God loves you, but He loves other people more.

You have a hard time loving others.

You have a hard time loving yourself.

You feel purposeless.

You feel as though you have no control over your life.

You turn to the Internet for pleasure.

You don't deserve the kindness of others.

You find yourself working to find acceptance.

You take anti-anxiety medication.

You have a hard time being happy.

You constantly strive to please your spouse but feel your efforts fall short.

You find your identity in your children.

A pastime seems to consume you.

You always keep an eye out for another position or place.

You feel driven to succeed.

Things are never as good as you thought they would be, so you live a life of disappointment.

You need to keep certain things about yourself hidden.

You're always working to contain your emotions.

Spiritual things trouble or upset you.

You have a hard time blessing others.

You find yourself constantly pointing out others' faults.

You don't think you deserve the good things you receive.

You're always putting yourself down.

You find it hard to rest.

You find it hard to trust anyone else.

You guard your heart so no one can get too close.

You find it difficult to submit to authority.

You always try to be different than other people.

You struggle with your sexual identity.

You live according to a strict set of rules.

Your motive for accomplishment is recognition.

You chose pleasures above principles.

You insist on maintaining a certain image.

You volunteer for everything.

You're a workaholic.

You crave intimacy but can't seem to find it.

You struggle when a loved one points out a weakness.

You have a hard time loving others.

You feel God is distant.

You believe your future is bleak.

You often worry about things you can't control.

You insist on your rights or what other people "owe" you.

You find it hard to make new friends.

You have never brought another person into God's Kingdom.

You hide behind others.

You don't have a dream of what God can do through you.

You repeatedly find yourself the center of controversy.

You're fighting an addiction.

You think you're unlovable.

You think it's impossible to please God.

You avoid situations that might reveal who you really are.

You think you don't belong.

You think you must always be in control.

You spend most of your time focusing on your faults.

You think no one else knows what you're going through.

You believe no one will take care of you but yourself.

You find joy in robbing other people of their joy.

Your family members distance themselves from you.

You choose truth and knowledge over love and life.

You don't have a place you call home.

You live with many fears.

You feel as though God never hears your prayers.

You blame others for the way you turned out.

You're bitter toward your parents and those in authority.

Your relationships are superficial.

You find it difficult to repent.

You don't manifest the fruit of the Spirit.

You always try to get others on your side.

You don't listen well.

You don't understand why others don't see your point of view.

You have no true direction in life.

You feel as though you're on the outside looking in.

You constantly puff yourself up in front of others.

You feel there's no use in trying anymore.

You find yourself saying yes when you'd like to say no.

You're always sure you're right.

You often worry about money.

You keep a record of who did what to you.

Notes

Chapter 1—The Orphan Heart

1. Donald Miller and John MacMurray, *To Own a Dragon: Reflections on Growing Up Without a Father* (Colorado Springs, CO: NavPress, 2006), 30.

2. "Last Words, Deathbed Statements," accessed 1/4/14, URL: http://www.corsinet.com/braincandy/dying.html.

3. "Ask the Doctor: Reactive Attachment Disorder," accessed 1/4/14, URL: http://www.internationaladoptionstories.com/rad.htm.

4. Jack Frost, *Experiencing Father's Embrace* (Shippensburg, PA: Destiny Image, 2006), 23.

Chapter 2—Spiritual Anatomy

1. John Eldredge, *Wild at Heart* (Nashville, TN: Thomas Nelson, 2001), 41.

2. Emory University Health Sciences Center (2004, March 16). "Study Finds Male And Female Brains Respond Differently to Visual Stimuli." *Science Daily*, accessed 11/7/13, from http://www.sciencedaily.com/releases/2004/04/040316072953.htm.

3. Robert Klara, "Something in the Air," *Adweek,* March 5, 2012, accessed 12/29/13, URL: http://www.adweek.com/news/advertising-branding/something-air-138683.

4. Bob Smith, *Dying to Live*, Chapter 10. (Waco, TX: Word Books, 1978), p. 96.

5. Watchman Nee, "The Spiritual Man," Part 8, Chapter 1, accessed 11/30/13, URL: http://www.worldinvisible.com/library/nee/sprtmnv3/part8chapter1.htm.

6. C. S. Lewis, *Surprised by Joy* (New York, NY: Harcourt, Brace, Jovanovich, 1966).

Chapter 3—Voiceover

1. William Paul Young, *The Shack* (Newbury Park, CA: Windblown Media, 2011, reprint edition), 91.

Chapter 4—Identity Theft

1. Frances Hodgson Burnett, *The Secret Garden* (New York, NY: Sterling Publishing, 2004), 12.

Chapter 5—Guilt Trip

1. Jamie Mason, *Three Graves Full* (New York, NY: Gallery Books, 2013), 73.

Chapter 6—Worried Sick

1. Hannah Hurnard, *Hinds' Feet on High Places* (Carol Stream, IL: Tyndale Momentum, Living Books ed.), 82.

Chapter 7—Fake ID

1. Frank W. Abagnale with Stan Redding, *Catch Me if You Can: The True Story of a Real Fake* (New York, NY: Broadway Books, 1980), 27.

2. *Catch Me if You Can*, 21.

3. URL: http://www.abagnale.com/aboutfrank.htm, accessed 12/3/13.

4. *Catch Me if You Can*, 292.

Chapter 8—Death Sentence

1. Sylvia Plath, *The Unabridged Journals of Sylvia Plath* (New York, NY: Anchor Books, 2000), 24.

Chapter 9—Redeemed

1. C. S. Lewis, *The Lion, The Witch and the Wardrobe* (New York, NY: Harper Trophy, 1950), 197.

Chapter 10—Reclaimed

1. Walter Wangerin, Jr., "Ragman," from *Ragman and Other Cries of Faith* (San Francisco, CA: HarperSanFrancisco, 1984), 4.

Chapter 11—Renewed

1. Laura Hillenbrand, *Unbroken: A World War II Story of Survival, Resilience, and Redemption* (New York, NY: Random House, 2010), 179.

Chapter 12—Restored

1. Corrie ten Boom with John and Elizabeth Sherrill, *The Hiding Place* (Grand Rapids, MI: Chosen Books, 1971, Billy Graham Crusade ed.), 205.

My Notes

My Notes

D6 | CONFERENCE

a family ministry conference
connecting **CHURCH** and **HOME**
through generational discipleship

D6conference.com

DON'T LET FEAR
HOLD YOU BACK.

MOVE BEYOND THE PAIN AND
STEP OUT INTO **FREEDOM.**

The author shares details concerning the **emotional and physical symptoms** related to the subject as well as ways to overcome these difficulties.

Readers will find **words of comfort and hope** through Scripture, examples from the Bible of those dealing with difficulties, and practical advice on surviving the difficult situation they are facing.

A **list of resources** is given to encourage further help where needed.

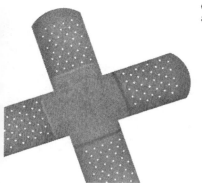

A DISCIPLESHIP EXPERIENCE
FOR THE CHURCH & HOME

D6
curriculum

- SOLID, **BIBLICAL** CONTENT

- SUNDAY SCHOOL/ SMALL GROUP CURRICULUM **FOR ALL AGES**

- DEVOTIONAL MAGAZINES FOR THE HOME

- FREE WEEKLY EMAILS PACKED WITH IDEAS FOR FAMILIES

CPSIA information can be obtained at www.ICGtesting.com
Printed in the USA
LVOW10s0403120514

385385LV00002B/3/P